Untied Marriage Knot

A Real Story

Unravelling the Threads of Betrayal and Finding True Love

KADAMBARI

From Royal Roots to Heavenly Harmony

Clever Fox® PUBLISHING

Chennai • Bangalore

CLEVER FOX PUBLISHING
Chennai, India

Published by CLEVER FOX PUBLISHING 2026

ISBN: 978-93-6707-858-7

A Heartfelt Dedication

I'd like to extend my deepest gratitude to ***Bill Perkins***
for his powerful prayer, pointing me towards God's love
amidst my loneliness and divorce.
Your kindness and faith meant the world to me.

Julia Salamonski, *your editorial skills and*
encouragement were invaluable
I especially thank you for joining hands with me
in this poignant memoir book venture,
and for your passion and dedication
to leaving it behind as a legacy.

A heartfelt thanks to ***Reena and Ajit Abraham,***
whose unwavering support and love
helped me to navigate through tough times.
You both stood by me when it mattered the most.

CONTENTS

PREFACE

UNTIED MARRIAGE KNOT

Beneath the Pulpit of Fake Vows

In this poignant memoir, the author explores a stark contrast between the sacred marriage knot of sanctity and the untied marriage knot of immorality.

THE STORY BEGINS

A handsome devout Christian suitor arrived from afar, with an intention of a marriage proposal to marry the beautiful Gospel Singer from a distinguished Hindu elite family whose lineage traces back to royalty.

Having met her personally, he was struck by her charming personality and instantly asked her, "Will you marry me? We both serve the same God, Jesus." His words deeply resonated within her heart, and she said, "Yes, I will marry you," feeling a bit shy.

The wedding bells rang, and they exchanged vows in an American Christian church. Sealed with a kiss their union was complete. They built a beautiful bungalow to live a life of luxury. Life was like a never-ending vacation for them, with exotic getaways, charities and galas. Their nights were filled with pink champagne, toasts, and sweet nothings.

But now it was her calling to fulfill God's commission, so she left immediately for the mission trips to share her talent through Gospel concerts in Churches, Crusades and Conventions. Bidding adieu to her loving husband, she took the first flight.

Upon her return back to her sweet home, she was shocked to see her husband's cold attitude. The man she once married was like a stranger to her. He ignored her, as if he had no time to spend with her or to know about the impact of her exciting International mission trips, her publicity, media coverage, and about the success of her gospel concerts to spread the fragrance of God's grandeur and glory.

Her dreams of a God-centered partnership shattered when she observed his behaviour, was all about self-gratification, being busy with his laptop until the late hours of the night, and not a shared mission of her expectation to serve the Divine God.

This stark contrast between the self-service ways, and God-centered aspirations led her to realize the truth. She then confronted him saying, "I know all that you have been watching till late hours of the night. We need to meet the church elder to resolve this issue." He shouted out and said, "Do you want to open the can of worms for me?" She replied, "Yes, I will tell the truth."

That moment marked the beginning of her nightmare. He transformed into a narcissist tormenting her by employing silent treatment, gaslighting, emotional abuse, and his pursuit for supply to erode her joy, peace, and self-esteem.

Heartbroken, she cried to the Lord, praying for his heart to change. She prayed, fasted, and sought God's authority and obedience over him. But he never changed, claiming, "I am, what I am. I will never change."

Then the Lord spoke to her through His word, "The way of the wind flows upwards for the wise that they may turn away from hell below."

She immediately booked her ticket, carrying a no-contact passport, packed her suitcases, and walked out with grace and dignity from his life, never to see him again—never, forever.

Then God in His perfect time unfolded her dream revelations into reality.

The petals of His promise unfurled. A breathtaking apartment with an array of 34 luxurious amenities was ready for her to take possession. The Shepherd of her soul then walked her in to inaugurate it. Overwhelmed by the beauty of the palatial apartment and by the magnitude of His blessings and love, she wept bitterly, falling at His feet, kissing, worshipping, and thanking Him for this luxurious gift. Then He lifted her chin and His eyes met her for a moment of spiritual intimacy and He vanished, leaving behind his love forever.

Love then became her legacy. She launched her Ministry Love-4ALL to add value to the NGO's Ashram's 140 vulnerable souls, the sick, poor, and the orphaned. Her apartment then became a hub of humility, where transformation and testimonies unfolded. Where she danced and sang praises loudly among the worshippers to enjoy and soak in the secrets of His spiritual treasures.

The atmosphere in her private bedroom was calm and blissful and emanated vibes in her soul that were serene, sacred, and peaceful. The morning view from her balcony looked gorgeous as the golden orb sun rays peeped behind the sky's blue curtains. The chirping of the birds, the sound of the cuckoo, and the soft gentle swaying of the breeze caressing her silently made her say, Ahah, Ahah, as she sipped the morning cup of coffee. Her heart melted, that moment, reminiscing the great purpose that God had achieved for her to have a luxurious life. "So is the word that goes out of my mouth; it will not return to be empty but will accomplish what I desire and achieve the purpose for which I sent it. Isaiah 55:11

Kadambari's book is a living testimony of God. It is based on Christian values and principles of love. Her unforgettable memoir echoes the beauty of His love amidst shattered dreams. Where despair yields to divine melody to raise her above the dead ruins of love.

Her skillful use of Biblical references, poetic flair, imagery, and emotional nuances elevate her narrative to be a masterpiece of contrary nonfiction.

Her soul-stirring book shines as a beacon of hope, illuminating biblical treasures and guidance to restore marital relationships. She invites all to embark on this glorious journey of hope and love. A beautiful gift from God that saves marriages. "A wife is a gift of God to a man, and the quality that man brings into the marriage is a gift to God." Proverbs 18:22

Learn to accept that gift your wife.

Ms. KADAMBARI ADVANI

CULTURAL AMBASSADOR OF THE UNITED WORLD

THE AWARD OF HONOR AND DISTINCTION

https://gardenofrenown.com/

CHAPTER 1

CHILDHOOD

Born with a Silver Spoon in My Mouth

I spent my childhood in Jaipur, Rajasthan, where I was raised. Rajasthan includes most of Rajputana, which comprises the erstwhile eighteen princely states. "Raja" in Hindi means (king or ruler) and "sthan" means (land or place); thus, Rajasthan is known as "the land of kings." It comprises most of the area of the large Thar Desert, which parallels the Sutlej Indus River valley along the border of Pakistan. Jaipur, known as the Pink City, is the capital and the largest city of the state. It is also known for its traditional colorful art of block printing, tie and dye, batik prints, gold-thread embroidery, and shimmering mirror work on fabrics.

Childhood, as I know it, was the most beautiful and luckiest part of my life. I was blessed to be born with a silver spoon in my mouth and had a luxurious childhood. My dad's business was booming at the time I was born. He had many different businesses besides the main transport business, in which he only had the monopoly. He had a fleet of buses that catered to the passengers traveling to different cities and towns in and around the Jaipur district. During the evenings, the entire staff sat around a large table at home and gave my dad an account of the day's earnings. The table used to be full of notes, rupees, and coins. I remember sitting at the table as a kid, each day playing with coins, separating them, and making piles for hours while my nanny watched over me.

I do not really recall if I had any toys, but I do remember a flat-faced doll in a long gown and a frilly hat that I always had in bed with me. Pink has been my favorite color since childhood. Every time I went shopping, I chose pink frocks, pink ribbons, and even pink socks. Being possessive and caring about my things, I hated anyone taking anything away from me. The one thing I was obsessed most with was my little cuddly pink blanket. I loved cuddling and sleeping in that "blanky" at night and dragged it all around the house during the day. No one ever dared to separate or pull that from me. For all knew how good I was at screaming as loud as I could to get my way. Dad, being a busy man, had no time to play or to be with me. I don't remember him carrying me on his shoulders or telling me stories. My mom was just the opposite; she was very warm, affectionate, and caring. Although she had a very hectic schedule, she always made herself available when I needed her.

My parents loved me a lot and provided me with the best things that I desired. Their belief was different than the traditional beliefs of Jaipur. They thought it was important for a girl to have the best education and to be independent in life. The best school in Jaipur to educate kids was started by Maharani Gayatri Devi of Jaipur in order to promote education among girls. Her school was known as the M.G.D. school. The Maharani's feisty spirit and boldness were the beginning for girls to break away from the purdah, the veiled face tradition, and to educate them. The purdah tradition was prevalent in the royal families and was part of the Jaipur legend. Her M.G.D. school was focused on breaking that purdah legend so that the kids from royal families could freely join the school. The M.G.D school worked on a British pattern and hired the most efficient staff from England. The M.G.D. fees were very high compared to other schools, making it difficult for common people to afford it. Admission to the school was also based on your status and your family background.

My parents wanted me to study at the M.G.D. school. I do recall the day when Mom got me all dressed up to go with Dad for an interview with the M.G.D. school principal. After entering the school, we were asked to wait in a posh waiting room for some time. Finally, we were called into the principal's office, where I noticed a charming, chubby woman seated at her desk. She stood up and greeted Dad. She seemed to be very warm and polite. She chatted for a long time with Dad and then asked me a couple of questions, to which I promptly replied. I think she was highly impressed and agreed to admit me, saying, "She surely will be a good M.G. Dian." We then stood up, shook hands with her, and left after thanking her.

Mom was extremely delighted to get the good news about my admission. She took me shopping and bought all the things needed for school, like shoes, dresses, stationery, and a school bag. I was so excited to get the school bag that I hung it on my shoulder and paraded around the house even before I began attending school.

The first day in the school was hard. I felt lonely without my mom or my nanny around, but I did well and didn't cry much. There were lots of other kids who probably felt the same way. In kindergarten, we learned the alphabet and numbers, played games, heard stories, had meals, and then were done for the day. It was nice to play with other kids.

After passing my first grade, I began to feel comfortable with teachers and other kids and was able to interact easily. The class was quite big, so the students were divided into four houses: red, orange, green, and blue. We had to wear the badge of the house we belonged to. I was in the blue house. The purpose of the different houses was to make the students more competitive in classes with other houses. Each wanted to score more marks for their house, which also worked for scoring in sports like running, high jump, hurdles, and other games.

The teachers were hard-working, dedicated, caring, and capable. Their main focus was on making each M.G.Dian an outstanding person in life and society. The method of discipline was very strict, and so were the rules and regulations for personal hygiene and cleanliness. We had regular checkups done on our nails, hair, teeth, and ears to see if they were clean. There was no excuse for being unclean, and punishments were severe and humiliating. I never got punished and was always neat and clean, except on one of those bad days when my teacher spotted my white tennis shoes splashed with mud during sports time. She scolded me for being a dirty girl and then put a black badge on me. The next day, during Assembly, I had to parade in front of the entire school with a black badge along with the other black badgers. It was so humiliating. I was ashamed, not only for myself but for getting minus marks for my blue house.

Another scolding I got from my Ma'am was when I addressed a senior student in my class by her name. It was a rule in school for younger M.G.Dians to address senior girls as "Jija," which means elder sister. It's been an age-old tradition of Rajasthan royalty to respect elders by not addressing them by name. Most of the girls in school were from illustrious ruling families, and some were princesses from the royal families; hence, we all were acquainted with this age-old cultural tradition.

The most memorable happy experience I had in school was my first duet dance. I vividly remember wearing a white printed gown and dancing with another girl who was dressed up as a boy. The song we danced to was:

"Where are you going to, my pretty maid? Where are you going to, my pretty maid?" "I am going for-milking, sir," she said. "May I go with you, my pretty maid?" "You're kindly welcome, sir," she said.

Another highlight of my childhood was when I was preparing to perform my first solo act, "Oh the troubles of the baby are very hard to bear," on our annual day celebration. I was excited and worked hard memorizing four pages of dialogue. I rehearsed religiously in front of Mom for days and waited in anticipation to perform the solo act, but unfortunately, my parents had planned a short excursion. I had no choice but to accompany them, contrary to my wishes. I was extremely shattered and heartbroken, and I remember crying all through my journey. I felt hurt as I had worked hard and missed this opportunity to display my talent.

Besides being artistic, I was good at studies. I liked every subject in school except arithmetic. As an exuberant and loud child, I was often the first to raise my hand and speak up in class. The shy girls, who all sat in their blue skirts and white tops with maroon ties, hesitated to speak out. Recess and lunch break were the times I enjoyed most. We played games like hide-and-seek and hop-skip-and-jump, and we ran around the garden catching and collecting butterflies. The school provided lunch for five days and brunch on Saturdays. The food provided was healthy, nutritious, and of high quality. There were plates, forks, spoons, knives, and napkins neatly laid out on the tables in the dining hall. The Ma'am sat at the end of the table to monitor our table manners. There was no excuse for leaving the dining room without folding the napkin and placing the fork and spoon in the center of the plate after having finished our meals. Brunches were great on Saturdays, but what I hated most was having an egg flip. Being hesitant and scared of my Ma'am, I often closed my eyes tight and just gulped it fast.

In addition to the school being an academy, it was also a finishing school and had a curriculum structure that was practical and meaningful both inside and outside school to build attitude, etiquette, belief, skills, discipline, and personality. It also gave the opportunity for kids to learn personal hygiene, table manners, and social interaction. The Maharani took a keen interest in making each M.G. Dian an outstanding person.

Besides loving my principal and teachers, the person I admired most was the Maharani. Her surprise visits to school thrilled all the students. We often would run to our classroom windows to have a glance at her. She mostly drove up in her red convertible car, flaunting her style and looking extremely gorgeous and ravishing. The annual day celebration brought a lot of excitement and preparation for Maharani's visit to school. The whole school was decorated with flowers and lights in her honor. As she walked in escorted by the principal, adorned in a French chiffon sari and decked in pearls, she stunned all by her beauty, elegance, and sophistication. As a custom, we all stood in a line to present her with a rose, which appeared to us like a dream-come-true fairy tale. The celebration ended with the cutting of a huge chocolate frosted cake, and the students honored the Maharani with messages, verses, songs, and dances.

Besides celebrations and festivities, the school had a lot of other extra-curricular activities, like practical theme weeks, to train us in painting, gardening, embroidery, and pottery. The sole purpose was to make M.G. Dian proud of the school and society. I was blessed that my parents made the right decision to educate me at M.G.D. After passing out of my fourth standard, I left the school. It was really heartbreaking to leave the school as I loved each day of my life while I studied there.

CHAPTER 2

FAMILY

The Beautiful Damsel and a Handsome Man

The structure of my family's foundation stood on the pillars of love. Below is the poetic form of my mom's amazing story that she shared with me of her teenage years.

"

The sun was setting spectacularly on Karachi, Clifton Beach.

Where teens and friends would often go to meet.

People thronged to view the incredible colors of the bay

As the pink, peach, sun, sank down for the day

Where families, tourists, and friends came to mingle

All those married, and those who were single.

When silver sand bathed in the humid light of the sinking sun

A damsel alighted from a horse-drawn carriage to have fun

As she joined her friends to stroll and race
Heads turned around to admire her face.
Proud and arrogant she looked at none
But still, she stole the heart of one.
It was that enchanted moment of twilight
Which arouses the yearning passion at night
To cuddle someone close beside
Just to lay the troubles aside.
That special moment when sun and sea become one
Your heart throbs that you have someone
Then the world seems to be infinitely divine
Just to believe someday she will be mine
As the horse carriage drove the damsel far away
His heart sank and he started to pray.
The flashes of her beauty came floating at night
He was sure it was love at first sight.

”

The man then tried to chase the damsel, who drove away in the carriage. His heart cried, and he hankered to meet her. Later, he found her whereabouts and started demonstrating his love. The damsel started receiving anonymous love letters and flowers. The romance was nurtured by his helpful maids, relatives, and sympathetic friends who empathized with the man's yearning to win her over. The naive and young damsel was finally carried away by his charm. The relationship blossomed and grew intense as they fell in love. Then they eloped to leave the town just to get married and settle down. The beautiful damsel was none other than my mom, and the handsome man, my dad.

After the discreet marriage, the rumor mills started grinding. Eloping was unheard of and unacceptable since they were part of the conservative generation. Mom was ostracized by her family for quite some time, which was very hurtful and humiliating. As time passed, the furor died off, and the family accepted them. As the saying goes, blood is thicker than water.

My Mom and Dad were two different personalities. My Dad's life revolved around business and its activities, while Mom focused on family and kids. I did not really bond closely with Dad, but I shared the most amazing relationship with Mom. I treasure every moment of my life that I spent with her. She was the most powerful driving force in my life. She stood beside me through thick and thin, making herself available for me despite her hectic schedule.

Her life reflected the love and passion she had for the family and the elders. Her truly endearing quality was love and sacrifice. She selflessly gave her time and support to family and friends. She volunteered to pay school fees for the poor to educate the needy kids. Being fluent and versatile both in English and French, she had students come over to study at our home. Mom was the most admired person in my life. She was classy, sophisticated, intelligent, and, above all, very beautiful. There were lots of social activities and interests that kept her busy. Besides being at parties and functions, she often spent her evenings with Dad at the club. The activities she enjoyed most were playing chess and watching polo.

The time I enjoyed most with her was when she took me out for treats at my favorite restaurants. Oftentimes, she would sneak into my bed at night and cuddle me while sharing her childhood stories. She was the seventh child amongst ten siblings. All her siblings were highly educated. Most of her brothers later made it big in life. Uncle Dowlat was the editor of the top newspaper. Uncle Manik was a criminal lawyer and, later on, was designated to be the Consul General of the Philippines in Mumbai. Uncle Arjun was a businessman who later gambled away his wealth on races and friends. Mom's eldest brother, Dr. Ranjit Shahani was a prominent author and an Oxford University professor in English Literature in England. He married the Philippines Senator Letitia Ramos Shahani, sister of the former President Fidel Ramos of the Philippines.

I do recall one of the scary stories she shared with me about Uncle Ranjit.

The story begins:

It was a dark, sultry night when the entire neighborhood was asleep in bed.

Suddenly, late in the night, a man walked towards the house and knocked at the door. Hearing the knock, the doctor was awakened and reluctantly got up to open the door. A strange-looking man stood in front of him, dressed in a long, black coat and a black hat. He said, doctor, my wife is in labor pain; I request you to please accompany me. I will pay you more than you can ask for." The normal instinct and uneasiness about seeing the strange, weird-looking man late in the night repulsed the doctor and made him flatly refuse the man. But the man, being persistent, persuaded and pleaded with the doctor and said, "My wife's condition is critical; her life is in your hands. Please save her."

Feeling a sense of responsibility and courtesy, the doctor finally agreed to go. The man then waited for him in the long, six-horse-drawn carriage while he got ready. As soon as the doctor came and sat opposite the man in the carriage, it pulled itself back onto the highway. The horses started running towards the isolated outskirts of the town towards the uninhabited land. Seeing the unusual location and solitary surroundings, the doctor felt his heart sinking. Soon, the thick dark clouds blotted out the stars and masked the full moon. The carriage kept racing and shaking through the thick of the forest as horses galloped over the crooked ground of stalky dead trees through the marshy area of the land. The dark silence of the night, the croaking frogs, the whizzing chirr of insects, and the thundering of the clouds sent chills across the shivering body of the doctor.

The squeaky carriage then rattled over the broken path; whizzing wind brushed across the doctor's face, which looked aghast, but he spoke not a word to the man. Ultimately, the carriage turned off the dusky trail and followed a forlorn, lonely, muggy lane. Then, making a screeching sound, the carriage stopped near a haunted, shattered, dimly lit house with no houses around. As the doctor entered the house with the man, the lights suddenly flickered, and the atmosphere became dingy. Each step made him hear the creak of the clear floor. As he walked farther, the room door ahead of them swayed open on its own, and he heard a loud gurgling noise that scared the bejeezers out of him.

As the doctor directed his gaze towards an unusually ugly woman in bed who looked like a demonic crockadillapig, he was awestruck and paralyzed with horror. The strong winds gushed across the doors and windows, and the dim lights flickered. The man said, "This is my wife; please help her deliver." Each gasp of breath he took made the doctor's stomach churn as he walked close to help her deliver. Believing something weird was going to happen, he began to cower. As the lady screamed and growled to push hard, the endless stream of grotesque, ugly, elfin creatures that looked like goblins got out turn by turn and jumped on the table beside the bed that was stacked with clothes. Each creature, in turn, put on their clothes and ran out of the room. It was the doctor's most tremendous experience of genuine visceral horror, both on the surface and much, much deeper than one can ever dream of.

He could no longer stand, staying in the very epitome of darkness and was physically and emotionally drained. As he wiped his stained hands and sweaty face to leave, he sensed he was not alone but that someone or something was stalking him to the carriage. The husband accompanied him into the carriage, and the carriage raced away. Petrified and awestruck, the doctor was cringing inside the carriage with fear. The things he had touched and the unique stench he smelled were imprinted on his horror-struck mind.

As the carriage raced past the gigantic, spiraled trees, the husband lifted his hand and somehow plucked some branches from high off the trees. He then said to the doctor, "Thanks for coming. Please accept this gift." The doctor, watching the very act of the man's hand stretching so high to pluck the gigantic branches, was disarmed by shock. He said, "Thanks," to the man. The carriage then came to a halt near the doctor's residence. Even though the doctor was drained and exhausted, he dragged the heavy branches out of the carriage in fear. As he hurriedly walked toward his house, he heard a whizzing sound and saw the carriage vanish into thin air. Most of the branches were torn apart and scattered on the street, and while the few left, he unwillingly dragged them into his house.

Once he got into the house, he collapsed on the sofa, petrified and horror-struck, and immediately fell asleep. Early the next morning, he was flabbergasted to see that the branches had turned into gold. He could not contain his joy and woke his wife. She was exuberant but also bewildered when she saw the gold. Later, they searched the entire driveway and the street to see if other branches had turned to gold but had no luck.

This was one of the most unusual stories I heard from Mom. She narrated many other stories about her sisters who resided in Mumbai. Mom also made it a point to take me on a holiday trip during school vacations.

The thrill and excitement of being in Mumbai was like a little girl's dream come true. Being with my aunts and uncles was such fun. We often stayed with my favorite aunt, Rukmani Devi, who owned a three-story mansion, which she later converted into a commercial place in Bandra West known as the Marina Guest House. Since Mumbai was the center of Bollywood, struggling artists came from all over India to find success there. They all preferred to stay at the Marina, for not only did my aunt provide them discounted accommodations, but she also supported them financially. Many of those who resided at the Marina became successful producers, directors, screenplay writers, lyricists, cinematographers, and film stars. Thus, my aunt earned great respect for her contribution to the Bollywood film industry by supporting aspiring strugglers. Every artist that stayed there felt it was the luckiest place to be. I was luckiest of all, as I had quality time with all the celebrities who pampered, loved, and played games with me at the Marina Guest House.

After the Mumbai trip, family life and the atmosphere at home changed. Dad was always out on his business trips. Things seemed so easy and comfortable in his absence. I could do what I wanted and when I wanted at leisure on my own terms. There was no one to keep a tab on me or enforce the rules and regulations that I was supposed to follow. According to Dad's rules, I had to keep all my things in order when I returned from school. I was not allowed to play in the mud with the neighborhood kids. After having a snack and a little rest, I had to work on my homework with Mom. Then, I would get ready to go with Ramu, our servant, at 6:30 p.m. sharp to the children's park to play games. After that, it was time for supper, and I had to be in bed by 9:00 p.m.

Another rule was that we children were not supposed to take part in Dad's social activities. Being a real socialite, he threw lavish parties on our terrace almost every week. The guests invited were political figures, high-ranking police officers, and successful businessmen. The chefs prepared the best food - both vegetarian and non-vegetarian. Most of the cutlery set on the tables was made of silver.

Dad's routine at night was to enter our bedroom and check if I was asleep or was chatting with my sister. I was a very naughty kid and very curious, too. One day, I went with my sister to the kitchen to see the specialties the cooks had prepared for the party. My sister was scared to enter the kitchen, but I was a daredevil. I left her and headed all alone to the kitchen. I saw a lot of mutton patties and appetizers laid out in trays. I put out my tiny little hand, grabbed a patty, and ate it. The cooks saw me, shouted at me, and said, "Go to bed, or we will call your dad." I rushed back to bed, and to my surprise, I saw my dad entering the room. He came close to me and said, "Open your mouth," and I opened it. He smelled my mouth and said, "Did you eat a mutton patty?" and I replied, "No, I did not eat it." I got a hard slap on my cheek. That was the first time my dad ever slapped me.

The next day, he took me to Amber, a temple built by Maharaja of Jaipur, to show me "Bali," the religious act of live animal sacrifice. I was so terrified to see Bali that I started weeping and clung to my dad's legs. The horrible scene of the oozing blood and the headless, trembling body haunted me for months. The incident later left a great impact on my life and made me a total vegetarian.

Dad's rules irritated me a lot, and he made me do all of my chores, although we had servants to run our small errands. Mom also thought he was very hard on me. He wanted everything in order and in its right place, from pencils to shoes to books. All had to be perfect according to his instructions. I gave him the pet name of a retired Lt. Gen, which made my mom giggle a lot. Besides being harsh and demanding, he had another side to his personality. He was very religious, too, and highly respected in society. He contributed and supported lots of charities and foundations. His days started with worship in the temple and prayers in the evening with the family.

I do recall one of his visits to the temple on a Hindu festival day. It was Sunday morning, and he had plans to let me tag along. He came to my bedroom and shook me, and said, "Get up and get ready soon." His military command-like voice to get me out of my comfort zone bugged me so much that I stood up on my bed with a clenched fist, hands on my hips, and shouted at him in my loudest voice, "When I grow old like you, I will pray! Just leave me alone for now!" Then I jumped back into my bed and hid out of fear. That was the first and last time I ever yelled at him.

I could never figure out why Dad wanted to get his own way in my life. Curious about this, I confronted him once and said, "Why can't the servants do my job when they are paid?" He said, "What's the guarantee you will have servants all your life? I can afford to pay now, but not after your marriage." I was speechless and walked out of the room.

As time passed, I got accustomed to doing my own chores. I no longer felt as if Dad was having his own way in my life. Dad's priorities had changed as his business was flourishing in full swing. Everything turned around after that date, and there was no looking back. His business boomed, and he was flying high, being in a good mood.

CHAPTER 3

COLLEGE

My Naughty Pranks

The admission into the college in Jaipur was not an easy task. The students who achieved high ranks in high school were given priority. I had not achieved such high levels of accomplishment. However, the top ranking was not the only criterion that the college considered. The richest and most influential parents donated huge funds to the college, paving the way for their children to be admitted. Somehow, I also felt my father would definitely pull strings to get me admitted. I anxiously waited to hear the news from him until one day, he patted my back and said, "You have been admitted into the Maharani's college."

It was such a joy to get the good news. I was thrilled and rushed to my mom to share the news with her. She hugged me and said, "Now you are a young lady and no longer a school kid." I replied, "Yes, Mom." I understood what she meant. I had to be self-reliant and independent. Her words struck me strongly. Deep inside, I knew I had to be self-sufficient and ready to experience this new phase of my life. So I was very excited and thrilled with anticipation to attend the college. Finally, the long-awaited day arrived.

It was a bright, sunny day outside, and the cool breeze was blowing through my window. I was in my bedroom packing my things and getting ready to leave when suddenly I was overwhelmed by the inner joy of freedom. I realized I could now dress the way I desired and look the way I wanted. I dressed in my new lovely frock, left my fluffy hair loose, and was happy that I had been set free from the confinement of the previous school's uniform and the old traditional braided fishtail hairstyle. My mom then complimented me for my hair style and we left for the college.

There was a lot of activity going on when I arrived at the college that very first day. Lots of girls were standing in the corridors talking, laughing, and checking the bulletin boards outside the classrooms. I was nervous and confused by all that was going on around me. I did not know any of the girls at this college. I was but one among hundreds of girls. I searched for my assigned class, entered the classroom, and sat all by myself in the third row. The classroom started to fill up as girls came in and found places to sit. A plain-looking girl came and sat next to me. She smiled at me and greeted me by saying, "Namaste." The professor came into the room, and all of the girls stood up and greeted her in unison. She introduced herself and then called off the attendance roll. We then got right into our lessons. The day passed by quickly. I felt nervous and alone that first day, but still I was confident that the days ahead would be bright.

Over the course of the following days, I met and learned the names of most of my classmates. Most of my classmates wore a typical Indian dress or a sari. Most of them were much older than I was. I felt like a kid among them wearing my frilly smart frocks. They conversed with me in Hindi and not English. I spoke fluent English and was not accustomed to speaking in Hindi.

As months passed by, I felt very comfortable in my surroundings at the college. Most of the girls in the college liked me; some even complimented me, saying, "You are so cute." The professors also were loving and courteous. Although I had not developed any close friendships or clicked with anyone in particular, I was able to mingle with a certain group of girls who were extroverts, warm, and friendly. I was naughty and bold and no longer hesitated to show them my true colors. I must admit, I was a bit of a daredevil doing the things I did with them.

One day, while my professor was teaching, I stood up in the classroom with one of my smallest finger pinky pointed up in the air as the signal to be excused to go to the washroom.

The professor nodded her head, giving me permission to do so. I ran out in a jiffy to the shelf where all my classmates kept their lunch boxes, known as tiffins in Hindi. I opened all their tiffins, exchanged their meals, shuffled some of their good stuff into my tiffin, and dumped eggs into their tiffins. I then quietly entered the classroom and took my seat. When the class was over, we all left to have lunch.

The anticipation was unbearable as I waited for them to open their tiffins. The first one who opened her tiffin saw the eggs I had dumped in it, screamed loudly, and threw the tiffin back down on the table in front of the other girls. As others opened their boxes, they were struck with shock and amazement. I slowly opened my box and pretended to be startled like all the rest and asked, "How could anyone do such a thing as this?" They all chimed in their agreement by saying, "Yes, how could anybody do this?" It was very hard for me to control my laughter. I had so much fun seeing their facial expressions change. None of them ever suspected that I was the culprit.

About a week later, I told my classmates, "We need to find the culprit. If you don't find out who did it, then I will." As time passed, I thought everyone had forgotten about the episode except me. During one of my classes, I again left my classroom, messed with their tiffins, came back in innocently, and resumed my seat. I was so excited and thrilled to fool them again. I could hardly concentrate on what my professor taught that day. I was so anxious for the class to be dismissed for lunch. Finally, the class was over, and we left to have lunch. I was dying to laugh and could hardly control myself. As soon as everyone had sat down, they opened their boxes. I was very slow in opening my box, looking down, trying to hide my smirking face. Then I heard them shout, "How could anyone do this again?" This time, I could not contain myself, so I busted out laughing and said, "You all wanted to catch the culprit. Now, she has shown up once more and has gotten you all again. "They all caught hold of me, laughed loudly, and said, "You little devil, how can you be so naughty?" The story of my joke spread like wildfire in our classroom and throughout the college. It was the greatest prank of that year.

The thrill of that success was so immense that our whole group decided to pull a prank on the canteen owner. We plotted out a strategy for how to get the best of him. When we arrived at the canteen, some girls decided not to follow through with the plan because they were scared and said, "What if we get caught?" Others pointed at me and said, "She can do it." I felt honored and so excited that they trusted me to do the task. I should have felt nervous, but I jumped up from my seat and volunteered. We all walked up to the canteen owner and ordered samosas for each of us. A samosa is like a large triangular spring roll stuffed with potato and spice. When he motioned to us that our order was ready, I went to the counter to pick it up. I checked the packet, pretended to be upset, and said to him, "Sir, these are cold! Would you please heat these right now?" He took them from my hand and turned his back to me so that he could heat them on the stove. As soon as he had turned away from me, I sneaked up behind him, picked seven or eight samosas from his plateful on the countertop, and ran away. The owner didn't see all of us making off with our ill-gotten gains. The girls all complimented me, telling me what a good job I had done. We all gobbled up the samosas while not being able to contain our laughter.

I often wondered how I could have done such wicked, nasty things. It was such a shameful thing to do, but that was the thrill of the moment for me at that point in my life. I admit I was not yet done pulling pranks on other girls and professors, too. I was a good impersonator and possessed the ability to change my voice, tone, style, and mannerisms to mimic certain girls who had peculiar traits or habits. Soon, this became a pattern of entertainment for all. The whole class would laugh out loud at my antics, and even the girl I imitated had fun watching me portray her.

I recall one of my professors who walked in a peculiar fashion, bending to one side and holding an old purse under her arm. She spoke in a thin, high-pitched voice and wore low-cut blouses. She often came late to the classroom. On those occasions, I would run out of the classroom and make my entry, imitating her, tilting to one side with my blouse pulled down. The whole classroom would burst out laughing, clapping, and whistling at me.

No matter how many naughty, mean, or nasty things I did, everyone seemed to like me a lot. I think the primary reason was they thought I was a child at heart and had the courage to do the things that they could not do. As far as I knew, nobody felt humiliated when I mimicked them, but all took it in a stride. I continuously entertained my classmates, and I enjoyed the fun I had with them.

Even though I was naughty, I also had an innovative, artistic, and creative side to my personality. I was not athletic and had no interest in sports. I just loved dancing, singing, and doing theater. The college had lots of competitions and festivals for students to participate in and display their talents. The Intercollegiate Youth Festival was one of the most prominent ones held at the state level in the capital city of Delhi. The sole purpose was to educate students about different cultures, traditions, and art. The main emphasis was on folk dances, music styles, and presenting plays. Each of the colleges sent their most talented students to compete in different categories such as light music, classical music, classical dance, folk dance, drama, and poetry.

Our teachers had selected the best students in each of the categories to represent our college. I was thrilled to read my name included on the selected list. Although it was tedious staying late after class each day doing rehearsals, it was worth the struggle for a free trip to Delhi with friends.

The day finally arrived, and we reached Delhi, a city bustling with activity. The streets were clogged with cars, scooters, trucks, and buses. You could see auto rickshaws, bicycles, and pedestrians crisscrossing through the streets. There was such a hustle and bustle to it all. To me, it sounded like a great traffic symphony of car horns beeping out the melody of some great composition. As the college students arrived at the festival campus, both girls and boys were allotted separate sections to stay. There were eight girls in our group, and we were given a large room to share. After putting away our suitcases, we freshened up and set out to have our supper. As we entered the dining room, we saw a lot of girls and boys who had come from different states from across India.

After supper, we came back to our room. It was bedtime, so we all started to prepare for bed. I soon took off my frock and changed into my pajamas. The girls felt awkward undressing in front of each other, so I suggested that I would turn the light off for their convenience and switch it on when they were fully dressed. They all agreed, and I went over to the switch and turned it off. After a few seconds, I started saying, "Should I switch it on now?" Then they all screamed, "No, no, no, not now!" After a few seconds, I again said, "Now?" And they all screamed aloud, "NO!" At that exact time, I switched on the lights. It was so much fun watching them half-dressed, running here and there, hiding themselves, shouting and screaming, some taking off their tops, some even without tops. That's the time I said, "Wow! That was good stuff, a lovely free show." They replied, "Just wait. Someday, we will catch you and strip you nude. That will teach you to mess with us."

Everybody seemed to enjoy the Youth Festival, held at Talkatora Gardens in Delhi. Every girl competing in the festival was extremely talented and unique in style. The folk dancers of each state wore beautiful outfits, but I thought ours was the most colorful and gorgeous. The time came for us to perform a Rajasthani folk dance. We all wore colorful, long, swirling skirts decorated with gold and mirror embroidery, with a backless short blouse tied with strings. Our heads were covered with a beautiful long chiffon scarf full of fine gold embroidery. In addition to the wonderful costumes, we also wore heavy traditional shimmering jewelry like earrings, chokers, bangles, and anklets.

When our group was announced, the music started playing, and we took to the stage for our performance. It was such a wonderful feeling dancing in the stadium at night with colorful lights flashing on the stage. The most memorable moment of that day that left a great impact on my heart was to experience the joy of the thunderous applause we received after our dance performance. The auditorium was buzzing with the sound of clapping, shouts, and whistles. It was so humbling but very exciting to win the first prize for our college.

After a couple of days, the festival was over, and it was time for us to go back home. We all packed our bags and were ready to leave. It was difficult to say adieu and goodbye to new friends as we had developed a special bond. There were lots of tears, hugs, kisses, and contact information exchanges before we departed.

Our college had other optional activities like National Cadet Corps (N.C.C.). The purpose of the N.C.C. is to develop character, discipline, and leadership in all walks of life and to serve the nation. My choices and pursuits were contrary to the direction of being an N.C.C. cadet, so I preferred not to enroll in the N.C.C. program. One of my professors had a different opinion and pressured me to participate in the N.C.C. training camp. I was nervous and scared as I thought of the mess I would be getting into. Soon, the day came to leave for the camp. Initially, it was a lot of fun traveling by bus and viewing the lovely landscapes, mountains, flowers, and greenery. The bus was full of prospective cadets, and we sang songs while playing Antakshiri, a singing game where you compete with each other. One group starts a song and sings one line. The other group then must sing a line from another song whose title starts with the same alphabet letter where the first team ends the song. For example, if the first team sang, “I love you, Lord,” then the other team has to start a song that ends with the letter “D,” the last letter of the word “Lord.” It could be any other song, such as “Don’t forget me” or “Darling, you are so sweet.” We all enjoyed it and had so much fun playing this game, shouting and screaming at each other and simultaneously nibbling the snacks that the girls and the teachers had brought. The time flew by fast, and we soon reached our destination. I was amazed by the scenery as the bus pulled into the camp. I could see mountains, open fields, and forests that looked beautiful. But still, I was not happy being there. As I was alighting from the bus, I saw several neatly arranged rows of tents on the ground. Our professors then called us all together and assigned each of us a tent in which we would be staying. I was assigned tent number 4 to share with three other girls from my college. We were each provided with a khaki uniform, cap, shoes, mug, plate, and a thick, coarse blanket. When I entered the tent, I felt claustrophobic since it was small and low to the ground. Despite my being uncomfortable and overtired, somehow, I fell asleep that night.

Early in the morning, I was awakened by the sound of a loud whistle and a lot of commotion. As I got up from my bed, I saw girls running to and fro, getting ready for breakfast. Others were packing their bedding and placing things in order. I was hurrying to catch up with them, but they all left me in the tent and were gone. My problems started with my khaki pants being too loose, my shoes too tight, my socks too coarse, and my cap too old and shabby. I hurried to brush my teeth and to take a shower , but I was very late when I arrived for breakfast. Before I could even take a few bites, the whistle blew for the training to start. I was feeling so exasperated at being pushed hard to do these things that I didn't want to do. I had never wanted to come to this camp, and now I was already feeling miserable, both physically and mentally. I felt and looked like a vagabond wearing old clothes donated by some charity. This did not fit my style. I was not athletic and had never done any rigorous physical workout in my life. Somehow, I caught up to the other girls standing in line who were about to start their training. I kept observing them and copied what they did.

Since I was the only one there who had never done any of the exercises before, I caught the attention of the instructor. She noticed that I was not performing at the level of the other girls. She kept picking on me and scolding me. She started saying nasty things to me, like, "It is such a shame that after all this training for months, you are still unable to do normal routine exercises." The other girls giggled a lot at her comments actually, so did I, knowing that she was unaware of the fact that it was my first day and I had never been trained before.

After a few days of her sarcastic remarks, I decided I had to set the score right. The next day, when the morning whistle blew, I refused to get up. The associate officer entered my tent to inspect and started shouting at me and calling me a lazy lump! I pretended to be sick and said, "I have a severe stomachache." She took me to the camp Major, who was a medical doctor. He gave me some tablets to swallow and advised me to rest. The associate officer then forced me to gulp those tablets down, which was pretty frustrating for me to do, and then she left, disgracing me with a nasty remark.

I felt extremely miserable, lost, and lonely as I walked back to my tent. There was no one around. I felt hurt and depressed by the nasty comments of my instructor and the officer. I was starving, as I had not eaten anything since morning. I sat down on the floor and started weeping. Soon, I felt someone touching my shoulder. I quickly wiped my tears away and tried to pretend as if nothing had happened. I looked up and saw a lady with a large tiffin standing in front of me. She said, "Will you give this to Meera?" Meera was one of the girls sharing the tent with me. I nodded and said, "Yes, ma'am." She kissed me and said, "Enjoy the food," and then left. As soon as she left, my face brightened. It seemed like God had sent an angel for me. I pounced on the tiffin of food and had a wonderful treat. I felt peppy, and life looked so good to me once again.

Soon, I forgot all about the sarcastic remarks I had gotten from the instructor and the humiliation I felt. I was happy that all the insults turned out to be a blessing in disguise. After the hard day's work, when the girls returned to the tent, they saw the open tiffin with all the food laid out on it. They screamed with joy and said, "What's this party about?" I replied, "Just eat and enjoy." It was such fun watching them having a blast and nibbling while I shared about Meera's aunt's lovely gesture.

The next day, the same professor who had pressured me into coming to camp designated me to work for the night shift. I was thrilled to have this lovely opportunity to be out of the tiny, hot, congested tent. The fun was great, being out on the night shift with the other girls, walking in the moon's silvery light, and checking tents throughout the camp. I just felt relaxed and refreshed as the gentle breeze softly kept swaying over us. As we strolled around the tents we shouted, "Turn off your lamps and go to sleep!" We chatted, gossiped, laughed, joked, and shared so many things amongst ourselves.

As we walked ahead through the cool of the night, we passed by a tent tied shut with strings. The girls told me it was the canteen. I was surprised to hear we even had a canteen in the camp. We all stopped and tried to open the complicated strings, but we failed. The only option to sneak something to eat was to lie on the ground and slip our hand under the tent. W.O.W.! That just worked out great, we were able to lay our hands on biscuits, sandwiches, and wafers by grabbing them out from under the edge of the tent. We laughed and laughed as we ate and shared our ill-gotten gains with each other.

The following day, I still pretended to have a stomachache, and that night, I enjoyed fooling around. The next day, I decided to pull a prank and took a black eyebrow pencil with me. The idea I had was to paint mustaches and beards on the sleeping girls' faces at night.

When we assembled to go on duty, I told my friends about the plan I had. Everybody liked the idea. That night, we succeeded in painting mustaches and beards on many girls' faces, entering into their tent slyly and being careful not to wake them. I then suggested that we paint the face of the professor who had put me into this rut. The other girls were all scared, but I was determined to pull it off. I crept slowly and cautiously into her tent and succeeded in painting a mustache and beard on my professor's face. The next day, there was a lot of furor over who could have done this. The victims were blaming other girls in their own tents. No one even suspected that we were the culprits.

In the evening, we all gathered around the campfire to sing songs, play games, share jokes, and hear stories from our professor. The professor had decided instead to call a meeting to discuss the complaint she had received from some of the girls. She said, "I believe someone in the camp has crossed the boundary of good behavior by painting mustaches and beards on innocent girls sleeping in their tents." I want to know who did this thing." Many of the girls laughed out loud because some were unaware of the prank. She fired back, saying, "There is nothing funny to laugh about. I urge you to behave well and not pull such nasty pranks on each other." I watched my friends' faces blushing as I sat innocently during the meeting. I could hardly control my laughter. The other girls were scared even to make eye contact with me. They knew it would be very difficult for them to contain their laughter if they saw the feigned look of innocence that I tried to project.

I found the greatest joke for me was about the professor who was the victim of my face-painting adventure who never mentioned anything about her own face being painted. All through the meeting, the image of her beard-and-mustache-painted face with big rollers in her hair came in front of me like a vision. I had to fight so hard to control my laughter. So I made a really smart move by going to the washroom to laugh out my guts there. My other friends were stuck inside, and I am sure that really must have made it more difficult for them to control their laughter. Later that day, we played games, heard stories, and shared jokes with the professor, which gave us the freedom to laugh loudly and freely about our prank rather than at the jokes.

The last two days before the end of the camp were for participating in music, drama, and dance contests. Every group was represented by the most talented girl. All the performers were great and displayed different styles of music and dance. I did the Manipuri-style dance and was nervous and doubted whether I will have a chance to win. Finally, when the results were announced, I was surprised and excited to find out that I had won the first prize to make my camp feel proud. Camp was now over, and we all said tearful goodbyes to our new friends.

Back at college, I participated in various activities and rehearsals which started after classes ended for the day. It was difficult for other girls to wait that long for me as we all shared the buggy. There were other girls who came to college on bicycles, so I started to ride a bicycle instead of sharing a buggy. I knew that would save my other friends time, and they could get home early and not have to wait for me.

After a couple of days of riding my bicycle, I found out that it was a real nightmare. The boys from the Maharaja's College, which was across the street from our college, started following us when we left to go home after classes were over. It was difficult to ride the bicycle as they tried to topple us over with their stunts. Not only that, but some were very vulgar and pulled our scarves right off of us as we passed by. They would sing songs and say nasty things to us.

I told Mom about it and asked her to buy me a scooter to ride to college. She was very hesitant and said, “How can any girl ride a scooter in a place like Jaipur?” I replied back to her, “Only your daughter can,” and she smiled. After much pestering, she bought me a lovely red scooter. I was the first girl in Jaipur to own a scooter, and I felt so blessed to get it. I came and went from college at my leisure. All my classmates were so excited to see my scooter, and I was so happy to flaunt it in front of them.

The blessing of my scooter soon turned out to be a curse in disguise. I was so conspicuous riding to and fro from the college that everyone noticed me on the streets and around the boys' college. More boys than ever followed me, trying to race with me. Some even followed me as far as my home. That made me very nervous and scared. It was too much of a strain on me to deal with those cheap roadside ruffians. As the final exams were approaching, I didn't want to be hassled riding a scooter, so I gave it up.

My main focus now was to study hard. I did a lot of reading and concentrated diligently on remembering all I could. I stayed awake till late hours at night studying. All the hard work ultimately brought good results, and I passed with good marks. After completing my first year at college, I noticed a change in my attitude. The strain of the exams had made me a bit more serious than I had ever been. It was a lot of responsibility for me to study further.

Somewhere in my heart, I felt I could not take things so lightly as I had been doing.

After passing my intermediate classes, I enrolled myself in a Bachelor of Arts degree, which I passed with flying colors. I then entered the University of Rajasthan to study for a Master's Degree. I passed the first year of my Master's Degree program but, unfortunately, was unable to continue the next year. That year, Dad planned to move from Jaipur to Mumbai because of his business. I had to leave college, which was so disappointing and heartbreaking to me. A couple of months later, I found myself living in the bustling city of Mumbai.

CHAPTER 4

SOARING HIGH

Having the Best of Both the Worlds

Moving to Mumbai - the second most populous city in the world - was great. Mumbai is also known as the commercial and entertainment capital of India, and it has a population of approximately 20.5 million. Mumbai also offers abundant opportunities to people who throng there in search of bright careers and future prospects.

Knowing that Mumbai was the wealthiest city in India, Dad had already bought a lot of apartments and invested money in new projects, which he trusted would profit him in due course of time. I was very excited to be in Mumbai after a long lapse of time, and it reminded me of my childhood there. My aunts and uncles were thrilled to meet me and could hardly believe the kid they knew had grown up to be a charming young lady.

Life was initially cool and a lot of fun without any anxiety about studying or passing exams. I had no schedule to follow for each day nor any office job to run to. Meeting aunts and uncles and spending days with them was joyful and precious. We played chess and cards, went shopping, watched movies, dined out, and had kitty parties each Sunday. But that was just not the life I was looking for. As months passed, I was highly frustrated, bored, and extremely depressed. There was no purpose in my life. I desired to do something lucrative, develop some skills, or pursue my dancing or music career.

Dad had a big influence on my life, and I wondered why he did not let me complete my Master's Degree in Jaipur. By leaving the university, I lost my social life, college friends, and my lovely career as a dancer. Before relocating to Mumbai, I had already been recognized as one of the best dancers in Jaipur. I had started getting commercial assignments and bookings to perform at important events, functions, and celebrations.

I do recall a bad encounter between Dad and a noted top-notch film producer from Madras, who had visited Jaipur in search of talent for his new venture. The producer was in the audience and had witnessed my dance performance at the college's annual day celebration. Being highly impressed by my talent, he somehow managed to reach my residence the next day. He then asked Dad if he could sign me for his movie and make me into a big star. Dad was furious at him and threw him out of the house. But that was not enough; he even got upset with me and shouted at me, "Enough of your dance! I do not want you to dance again." I was shocked and hurt and cried my heart out. I knew I was talented. I was getting offers. I had a career. I loved what I did. Then why could I not do what I want? I knew other girls had no aptitude for dancing or talent and were being promoted and encouraged by their parents, but it was not so in my case. Dad never encouraged or promoted me.

Since Dad had prevented me from performing as a dancer back in Jaipur, I knew he would definitely not allow me to pursue it in Mumbai. He never thought dancing was talent but instead saw it as a cheap style of body display meant only for illiterate, lower-class girls. He had a mindset based on his traditional values and never desired dancing to be my career. His main intention in relocating to Mumbai was to search for a suitable match from an aristocratic family and to get me married. He often discussed with Mom about the eligible bachelors that he felt matched his requirements. This bothered me a lot. I was young and bubbly and possessed the basic skills to achieve success as an artist. I was not ready to marry some stranger so early in my life.

My sister was still studying in Jaipur. I felt lost and lonely and had no company at home. I thought there was no good reason for me to waste my life locked up in an apartment, brooding and whining. I started looking into the advertisements in the newspapers. Air India had an opening to hire air hostesses. I secretly sent in an application and was called in for an interview. I was ecstatic when I was informed that I was selected and would receive an official letter to start training within a few months. I was elated and could hardly contain my joy. I could see myself traveling all over the world. And kept imagining how great that life would be - seeing different places, meeting different people, learning about their different cultural traditions, tasting their yummy cuisines, and learning their languages.

At some point, I knew I had to share the news with my parents. I told Mom the whole story of how I managed to get this job. She was so happy and told Dad. He just got furious once again. He called me in and said, "So you want to be a sophisticated maid to the passengers, picking up their trays, plates, and even what they throw out." I was dazed and awestruck at his comment. I never looked at the job the way he did. He called it demeaning, degrading, and also risky. Ultimately, he talked me out of it. He was still making my decisions for me.

I was his daughter, after all, and I felt I could be quite a match for him. So, I didn't give up easily. I entered college to earn a diploma in advertising and public relations, and I got busy attending those classes. I liked those classes, as I had an aptitude for being a creative copywriter. The Advertising and Public Relations College was co-educational. The girls and boys were very cordial and friendly to each other. We socialized a lot in groups after college hours, visiting the cafeteria, going to movies, and watching plays.

On one of my visits to my friend's place for tea, I had the privilege of meeting both of her parents. While having a long chat with them, I learned that her dad was a prominent music Guru. I shared with them my belief in my talent in both dancing and singing. The Guru suggested that I sing for him. I was shy, very nervous, and hesitant to comply with the request, but somehow, I managed to sing. I was amazed by the compliments I got from the Guru when he said, "You have a voice that can make you a star." I was flabbergasted and excited and blurted, "Would you make me a star?" He smiled and touched my head, blessing me while I touched his feet, which is a Hindu tradition that shows respect for a Guru.

On my way back home, I was thrilled! I knew I had finally made the right decision and now would be able to fulfill the potential of the talent that I had if I worked hard. I soon became the Guru's protégé and started my training. I was elated, but Dad was not happy about my decision and refused to pay the tuition fees to the Guru. Mom was such a darling. She volunteered to help me, saying, "I will foot the bill; you just work hard." So, I put my heart and soul into working hard to achieve perfection.

The Guru trained me in classical music, which was really difficult. After a couple of years of training, I was all set to perform on stage. Things just got better and better for me. I started doing concerts with top artists and often shared the stage with them. Later, my Guru's health deteriorated, and within six months, he died. Coping with the news of his loss was immense. I was left without my best advocate and felt resentful about going back to my normal family routine. Over time, I gathered the courage to fight my own battles and worked myself into exhaustion by practicing religiously. The concerts were scheduled, and as an artist, I had an obligation to make sure that "The show must go on."

Fate had different plans, however, and opened a new door for me. A renowned singer approached me to perform at one of his concerts where his other protégés were supposed to share the stage with me. After the concert, he asked me if I would join him for his future concert assignments. That was the best thing that ever happened to me! I smiled and said, "It would be my privilege." I joined him and started doing concerts all over India. Then, I moved on to doing concerts in Dubai, Kuwait, Abu Dhabi, Sharjah, Hong Kong, and London. In the meantime, I received a lot of coverage in magazines and prominent newspapers, which helped me to gain popularity, publicity, and more assignments.

Mom sacrificed a lot by accompanying me everywhere I traveled. Dad was not in good shape and had breathing problems that I probably thought must have prevented him from accompanying me. It was on one of his business trips that he suddenly died of a heart attack. The news came in as a sudden shock which seemed incomprehensible. He was such a strong pillar for Mom to hold on to, and then, in a moment, he was gone. Dad's death was the hardest thing for us to cope with his loss and also to manage his business.

After his death, most of the properties were taken over by the renters who occupied them. Mom and I had no documents or ability to sue the renters to get back the ownership of our property. It was a rough phase of our life.

As time passed, I started my textile business and launched the "Sai Baba Textile Company." (Sai Baba was a saint whom most of the Hindus worshipped as one of their gods.) My textile company bought and sold shirt fabrics and also manufactured men's shirts and Bermuda shorts to export to Russia and to the American markets.

The business boomed and generated huge profits, but that was not sufficient for me.

I still desired to make it big, so I started tapping into other markets and searching for other options. I finally decided on the film industry, where real money flowed. Becoming a film producer was no joke. I had no contacts, no finances, no resources, no knowledge, or expertise. I just had a desire to produce a film. I always believed that "Thoughts are things." The thought that you think day in and day out is like a seed that grows and flourishes within you. The more you contemplate it, the faster the seed germinates. Soon, it finds its way out, guiding your spirit and finding ways and means to flourish and fulfill your dream.

I ultimately found a way to pursue my desire to be a film producer. I luckily got to know of the large L.B. Bank that financed most of the Bollywood film industry producers in Mumbai. I began searching for means to approach the bank and for the skills that I needed to convince the bank authorities into commitment. After a lot of research, I was ready to meet the chairman of the bank. The meeting went well, but I still had to comply with several tough requirements. The chairman needed confirmation letters from the potential main stars in my cast, a confirmation letter from the director, plus a copy of the script for approval before the bank could consider my application.

That was a really difficult assignment. After months of hard work, busy schedules, endless meetings, and much negotiation, I finally succeeded. I placed the star cast confirmation letters in front of the chairman, who was pretty astounded at my achievement. I believe I convinced him that I was resilient, diligent, dedicated, and skilled at my job. I received an initial confirmation but had to fulfill other requirements before the bank would actually finance my production. It took me two more exhausting years, working day in and day out and spending all my personal funds to finalize the post-production team. I now knew there was a lot of hard work in store for me as a producer. The producer must shepherd the film from conception to completion and beyond and has the final responsibility for every single small detail of film production. That same producer must be able to control production costs, maintain effective relationships with the director and post-production team, and have the knowledge of how to edit both picture and sound. Then, the same producer should be able to oversee the recording of the soundtrack, in addition to visual effects. Finally, selling territories, distributing and publishing the film to its final release.

It was almost too much for me to handle. I felt like an ant who was burdened to carry a mountain. There was no turning back, so with a lot of prayer and hard work, I ventured into production. Finally, the blessed big day arrived, and I launched my film under the banner of "Kali Maa Production." (Kali Ma means the "Dark Mother" and is the Hindu goddess of creation, preservation, and destruction.) That was the happiest day in my life, when the clapperboard hit and the assistant shouted, take one, shot one, camera rolling. The shooting then started, and my joy knew no bounds. After the shift was over, sweets were offered to all, followed by a lavish party. Shooting was actually really fun. I enjoyed visiting studios, meeting artists, working on scripts, searching outdoor locations, and planning schedules. Even though I was already a successful businesswoman and a singer, the overpowering sense of achievement as a film producer was still like an extra feather in my cap.

CHAPTER 5

MY DOWNFALL

I Had it All and Lost it All

Having achieved all I desired and dreamed of, I thought I was the luckiest person in my life. But I forgot that happiness is seasonal. It is like a butterfly: the more you chase it, the more it will elude you and later fly away far to be gone forever.

Life was a thrill every moment, and each day brought new surprises for me. I enjoyed each day of my life being happy, and everything was perfect.

The film progressed according to the artists' available dates. The shooting schedules were completed as planned. However, the time gap between planning and doing the actual shooting was not sufficient for me to manage my business and also take leave for concert trips. My textile export orders were pending. I had been unable to meet with the directors of other textile companies to procure materials and complete other business transactions. But after a couple of meetings and discussions, I somehow managed to sign the agreement. I was delighted to get the huge order to manufacture thousands of shirts for the Russian market. The agreement included a requirement to deliver shirts to the textile company on a fixed date to enable them to export the consignment.

I felt I had to move quickly, and having an A-type personality, I wanted to achieve the maximum amount of activity in the minimum amount of time. Soon, the fabric arrived at the factory, and my hired staff was put to work. The machines started rolling, and we began sewing shirts without collars since the brand tags had not arrived from the textile company. After a long delay and much persistence on my part, the brand tags arrived. Finally, the shirts were completed, and I received a call from my factory to come and inspect the consignment before it could be dispatched.

When I approached the factory, I was shocked to see the whole area blocked off with red police tape and all traffic being diverted to another route. I wanted to enter the factory and argued with the police to let me go in, but they refused. They explained that the area had been sealed off due to a bomb blast that occurred the previous night, damaging property and killing innocent people. I was devastated and petrified and felt completely defeated.

I waited desperately for days to know the outcome of the bomb blast and the amount of damage done to my consignment. Soon, things cleared, and I rushed to the factory to find out if my consignment was safe. And was ecstatic that all the stuff was safe. Then, I immediately called the textile company to take delivery of the consignment, and they flatly refused, saying the Russian market had canceled their order due to the shipping delay. Since my order was completed even before the bomb blast had occurred, I refuted their statement and accused them of purposely not sending the brand tags so they could delay the order. The tussle went on for a long time without a positive outcome for me. I felt controlled by time and urgency. I had a deadline to clear the goods from the factory before I was charged rent for storage. I was in a great dilemma. Finally, I had to allow the textile company to take the consignment without paying me a dime, and I also agreed to pay the wages to the laborers out of my own pocket. All my efforts and hard work had gone down the drain. My heart sank, and in sullen silence, I calculated the loss I had to bear.

At the same time, the shooting schedule of my film was fixed, and I had to push myself hard to get out of my depression. The movie scene was a wedding, which involved fifty junior artists besides the main stars. It was one of the most expensive schedules. My highest priority was to get the money from my banker. When I got to the bank, I was shocked to learn that the manager failed to keep his commitment and refused to give me the check. I had no time left and tried frantically to get my money to proceed with the shooting.

Now, I had to generate funds for the next shooting schedule, but the only option I had was to sell my unfinished film to the distributors. The film was more than half complete, then I arranged for a trial show for my distributors. The response was immense, and the film was highly appreciated. The deal was closed, and I went ahead with my next shooting schedule.

On my next visit to the bank, I was pretty amazed. Most of the staff was missing, and the chairman had gone overseas. The manager informed me that I needed to delay the shooting until the chairman returned. Months passed. The film production was at a standstill, and the chairman was unavailable. I had lost my patience and reported back to the bank to discuss my problems with the manager. He ultimately handed me a check for half the amount they had committed to me earlier. I argued a lot with the manager, stating that the amount was insufficient to meet my shooting expenses. He then suggested that I wait a few months more until he could arrange for more funds. In desperation, I reshuffled the schedules to shoot scenes that involved the junior artists in order to reduce my budget. Early in the morning, on the next day of my shoot, I heard the bad news that my main character artist had expired. That meant I had to spend more money to rewrite the script to explain his absence from the film. The shooting was canceled to pay homage to the artist, and that was an extra addition to my previous losses.

I felt sorry for myself as each day had more bad news in store for me. My condition seemed exactly like Job in the Bible. The only difference was that Job had the Lord Jesus, the true living God, to lift him up after his downfall and reward him in double measure. I had only my Hindu gods to whom I turned. I did everything under the sun to change things around. I visited temples and prayed to all the different gods that we Hindus normally worship. I fasted and paid money to each and every sadhu and pundit to perform rituals, but every effort failed. Nothing worked, and none of the gods came to my rescue.

Time was marching on, one endlessly long day after another in which everything was essentially the same. I had to dig deep down to find my strengths and weaknesses. I was not ready to quit or give up my dreams after putting in so much effort and money. I realized only fate could change my financial situation, but I was still rich in my talent and possessed the ability to succeed as a singer. I started devoting more time to music and doing more concerts. I also created an album with Shri Anup Jalotaji, one of the greatest religious bhajan singers in India. The songs that the album contained were praise and worship for Sai Baba, a Hindu saint whom most Hindus worshipped as a god.

During this turmoil, I often remembered Dad and his influence on my life. I realized he knew exactly how difficult it would be for me to fight the battles of my life alone. His plan for me to be married now seemed to have been the best choice for me. The prolonged tension and the fatigue of the unfinished projects pushed me down into a state of depression. Mom was worried and wanted me to take time to recuperate from my mental stress. She suggested that I needed to change my priorities, change my daily routine, and adapt to a new lifestyle. After much coaxing, I started going out to parties and tried to socialize with her friends. At one of the parties, her friend Sona suggested to Mom that I should meet an eligible bachelor she knew who could be the right prospect for me.

So, Sona and her husband arranged a meeting with this man at the Sea Rock Hotel and came to fetch me and my sister. As we entered the hotel restaurant, I observed an elegant, handsome man seated with another guy. As we approached, they both stood up and greeted us, and we exchanged pleasantries. The evening started with wine and appetizers. We all chatted for a long time, discussing and exchanging views about our business and career experiences, and then moved on to other interests and hobbies that each of us had. Later, the delicious supper was served, followed by a mango ice cream.

Cupid's arrow had struck, and Chintu was extremely fascinated by me. However, it was different for me. I was not enamored by him, although he was both classy and posh and held a high position as the managing director of a top stainless-steel company in Mumbai. I was still focused on my little world of ambition and my need for success. I was unable to think beyond that. All through the evening, I noticed that Chintu had a real talent for eye contact and flirting. His message became clear when he picked up a red rose from the table and presented it to me. As we departed after supper, he drove off in his Mercedes while Sona and her husband dropped us off at our residence.

A few days later, an excited Sona called Mom, informing her about Chintu's keen interest in meeting me again on Saturday at the Holiday Inn. All four of us met again with Chintu and his brother at the hotel. The ambiance there was classy, and the candlelit poolside restaurant had a great view across the seashore. As we sat at the table, the lilting melody of the romantic music mingled in our ears with the whistling sound of the wind across the sea. I observed several couples snuggling and many more dancing on the floor. The waiters served us wine and appetizers, which were later followed by a delicious meal. I was pretty relaxed as I chatted with Chintu, and suddenly, the singer announced, "This song is to wish Chintu and his fiancé a happy engagement." The waiters walked in with a large cake and brought it to our table. The guests at the other tables clapped and cheered us. I was awestruck and dazed. Suddenly, Chintu got up from his chair and escorted me to the dance floor. I asked him, "What is all this that's happening?" He laughed aloud and said, "Seeing is believing, but this is just the beginning." Then he snuggled me close to him as we danced. I was extremely shy and could hardly believe this was happening to me. The evening finished equally well. We had supper, and then Chintu took hold of my hand to cut the cake with him. Before departing, we exchanged numbers, and then Chintu came close to me and pecked me on my cheek to bid me goodbye.

Once I got home, I could hardly sleep. I thought of Chintu's love as a strong wave that struck me unawares and carried me away. I had no option or say in the whole matter, I thought. But admired his courage in presenting his romantic proposal to entice me into a commitment. I was not in love with him, but I enjoyed the royal treatment he gave me and his style. After that evening, my phone never stopped ringing. Initially, Chintu would dial my number and not speak but play romantic songs for me to hear. Then he started doing all kinds of different stunts, surprising me each time. He was peppy and full of joy and engaged me in conversation each night for hours.

All my life, I have preferred a man who treated a lady with respect. The one who kept his dignity by not being physical or vulgar in his actions or conversation. Chintu fit the bill, which made our relationship romantic and exciting. Being involved with him diverted my mind and helped me a lot to get over my business and financial problems. I soon realized love is like a tonic that heals you mentally and fills your life with joy. To win my heart was like a challenge to him. He made the courting game long and exciting. We went for long, romantic, moonlit drives, went to derby races, watched movies, and met at the best clubs, hotels, and restaurants. The only thing that made me a bit uncomfortable was when he made a lot of public displays of his affection. As time passed, he won my heart, and we fell deeply in love. His family had found out about our relationship and objected to it but failed to break us up. They insisted that he should leave me and marry the girl of their choice, or else they would take action to eliminate me from his life and disown him from their entire estate. All this was painful and disgusting. I had my self-respect and dignity and was not ready to stoop so low as to fight with his family. Instead, I opted to break off my relationship with him. I wanted to move on and didn't want the past to flood my present. Months passed, and Chintu's calls kept ringing, but I opted not to answer them. He sent flowers and messages that just tore my heart apart, but I still stood firm and did not give in. I was depressed and frustrated as I searched for peace. I focused my mind back on my business to keep myself occupied and kept on chasing the banker for funds. My income decreased, and my expenses increased. My personal funds were nearly exhausted, and I could no longer afford to pay my film production staff out of my pocket. I decided to confront the manager and met him at his office. I explained my situation to him, and he replied not a word but placed a sheet in front of me. As I read the sheet, I was shocked. The government issued a notice to shut down all the private banks effective immediately. I was speechless, and he said, "Our banks have been shut down, and we can't finance you further." I left the office heartbroken and shattered, knowing there was no way I could complete my film now unless I started all over again to find a new financier.

I was exhausted and not ready to face more struggles. Back at home, Mom was not doing well and needed a lot of care. Soon, she became weak and dehydrated and had to be admitted to a private nursing home. I preferred to stay with her at the nursing home so I could be by her side. Late in the night, the nurse knocked at the door as usual, and I observed Chintu entering the room following her. The maid at my home probably answered Chintu's call in my absence and gave him the information about my whereabouts. I was amazed to see him, but I really felt comforted in my heart to have him beside me. Mom was on medication and was fast asleep. He hugged me and cried, and I was totally confused. I loved him and needed him, but I wanted to get over him. There was not much for me to say, for he could see all that was written on my face. As he departed, he touched Mom's feet, and I asked him to promise me that he would not call or see me again.

But he answered, "No one can stop me from seeing you," and then left. After two days, Mom recovered her health and was discharged to go back home.

Time passed, and I didn't hear from Chintu again until my doorbell rang late one night. We were all in bed. The maid peeped through the main door and informed me that Chintu was at the door. I asked her not to open the door. He kept ringing the bell and banging on the door. Afraid that he might wake the entire building, I asked the maid to let him in. I quickly got dressed to face him. He stood and hugged me and said, "I can't live without you. I want you to marry me right now." I explained to him that it was impossible to marry without the prior consent of his parents, but he was adamant that it was his last chance to marry me because his parents had planned to marry him to another girl.

He insisted we should go to the temple and marry right then. Ultimately, after much persuasion, I got ready, and we left for the temple with my sister. The temple was closed, and the pundits had already retired. Chintu used all his influence to open the temple doors. The main pundit woke up and summoned the other pundit who would perform the marriage ritual. We waited for hours for the pundit to arrive with all the stuff needed for the ritual. Finally, the oath ceremony was performed, and then we were asked to put garlands around each other and then Chintu took sindoor, a traditional red powder, filled it in the parting of my hair, and put a dot of it on my forehead. We then signed the marriage documents presented by the pundit and were pronounced married. It was early morning when we came home. Then Mom greeted us, and we both touched her feet and took her blessing. It was a real-time of joy for the family as we took photographs, chatted, laughed, joked, and enjoyed being together.

Chintu's disappearance from his house late in the night made his mom frantic, and she sent her driver to my residence early in the morning to see if he had deceived her and was back with me. The driver reported back to her that he was with me, and she instructed him to get Chintu back home immediately. I asked Chintu to leave, but only after much hesitation did he finally leave.

Chintu's parents created a big problem for him after he left my home. They insisted he spend some time with the girl of their choice. He was adamant that he could not do it, but to please his parents, he met the girl a few times. The next time he left home was on the pretext of meeting the girl, and he ended up at my residence instead. He narrated the whole story to me about his parents' manipulation and their plan to get him married to the girl of their choice. Initially, I thought he was kidding me, but I soon realized he was serious when he handed me the name and telephone number of the girl.

I called the girl and told her that Chintu and I had been in love for years and that we were married. She wept and said, "That's not true. He is my fiancée, and our marriage date is fixed." I asked her to speak to Chintu, who told her to come and check the marriage documents. All this created a big furor. The girl's parents and Chintu's parents had sent the wedding cards to invite guests from all over India and abroad. The Taj Mahal Hotel rooms were already booked for their guests, and the Turf Club was the wedding venue. The bride's parents had purchased the huge dowry and jewelry. Moreover, both the bride and Chintu's parents finalized all the other necessary arrangements for the wedding. After checking my marriage document, I found that Chintu's parents had no option but to postpone the wedding. Chintu's parents were furious at their son and threatened to disown him from their entire estate.

During those times of trials, my dearest Aunt Rukmani Devi of Marina Guest House was brutally murdered. Before we could get over her loss, my darling mom's condition started deteriorating, and one month later, she passed away peacefully in my arms. Our sorrow at Mom's death was incapacitating, and our grief inconsolable. Her absence and loss created a huge void in our lives. We all had to face the harsh reality of life, knowing that death was unavoidable but a part of life's end. We fought our emotional battles, mourned and consoled each other, being left with our own scars to mark the void. The choice we had was to move on or not. Gradually, the great healer called time did lessen the harshness of our pain.

Chintu, while aware of my mental state due to Mom's loss, didn't want me to face more problems and threats created by his family. He warned me that his family had hired someone to remove me from the scene. He was concerned and protective and begged me to flee immediately from Mumbai. I was adamant and not ready to budge. Ultimately, I succumbed to his wishes, however, and planned to leave for England. He then dropped me at the airport, and felt that I would be safe there. He promised that everything would be sorted out in due course and that his parents would finally cool down before I returned.

My friends and hosts in England treated me like royalty. They took all measures to please and entertain me in order to help me get over the tragic loss of my mom and aunt. They were upset about the new threat I was facing due to Chintu's parents and were very concerned and protective, consoling me that soon this bad phase would pass away, and I would be blessed to have a wonderful life with Chintu. But destiny intervened.

It was that fateful day of June 23 when I got a call from my sister informing me that Chintu had been ill and had been hospitalized. I asked her, "Why was he admitted to the hospital?" But she was unable to explain that. I hung up and knew something was terribly wrong, so I called Chintu's residence. The maid picked up the phone, and I asked her to put Chintu on the line. She was sobbing and replied, "Chintu jumped from the ninth floor of his building and committed suicide."

I started shivering and became desperate to leave for Mumbai. My friends put me on the first available flight there. When I reached Mumbai, my sister received me at the airport and hugged me as I wept bitterly. She knew I had gotten the news of Chintu's death.

I cried my heart out for days and could never stop grieving the loss of Chintu because I could never stop loving him. I remembered the comforting words that he had whispered to me after Mom's death.

If tears could build a stairway
and memories a lane,
I'd walk up to heaven
to bring your mom again.

But now he also had deserted me and was gone, leaving me behind, broken and shattered. I needed strength to rise up again. It was at that moment I realized God doesn't promise gain without pain, joy without sorrow, nor sunshine without rain. He does promise strength to live each day and light to show us the way. I wanted someone to give me strength and to show me the way, and my search started for that God who is the way, the truth, and the life.

CHAPTER 6

MY ENCOUNTER WITH JESUS

That Changed the Course of my Life

I struggled within myself to find the true God, who would show me the way, erase my hurtful past, and give me the strength to cope with my grief. Grief doesn't disappear because the loss itself doesn't disappear but leaves a gaping hole inside. The loss of my loved ones had overwhelmed me to the point of losing interest in life. The life that had cheated me of my share of joy. I was also done visiting different temples, doing rituals, fasting, and praying to various deities, but all was in vain. I was lonely and lost and looking for something deeper, long-lasting, and eternal, for a relationship with God who would love me unconditionally, eternally, and make me complete in Him. I wanted to get back on track to regain myself. Depression had killed the very essence of me, and my eyes had exhausted all their tears. I knew in my spirit I couldn't let go of myself in doom by lying down in a pit for months. I needed to lift myself again. Thus, I declared belief in myself, knowing my inborn capacity, and decided to change everything around me.

The next day, I went for an evening walk, and while returning, I read a banner outside a bungalow that read, "Sometimes God lets you hit rock bottom so that you can discover He is the ROCK at the bottom. The words struck me, and I kept praying that I needed to discover that ROCK, but instead, the ROCK had already chosen me before the foundation of the earth to be a vessel of His honor for His glory. That was revealed to me when I attended a born-again Christian prayer meeting suggested by a lady named Padma, who had called me up earlier after the sad demise of my mom and aunt to pay her condolences. But instead, with a new twist, she started calling each night, convincing and selling me her true living God, Jesus. He is the One you need now, and He can only change things for you. So, finally, having the growing expectation of meeting Jesus, I reached the apartment where the Hindu prayer groups were praying, making unfamiliar sounds, which I was unable to discern. Then, as I walked ahead, I observed the prayer room filled with women from different castes seated on the floor, all wearing different types of colorful Indian dresses. They all were praying with their eyes closed and heads covered. Some had their hands lifted to heaven, and others bowed down to the ground. No one observed me as they were all engrossed in prayers. I was confused and could not understand what sort of prayer that was. There was no priest, no ritual, no incense, no flowers, nor a photo of Jesus. Seeing no place to sit, I quietly sat near the entrance of the room, not to disturb anyone.

I waited for a while, closed my eyes, and started praying to Jesus in my heart, saying, "Jesus, I have come at your feet, God, broken-hearted, shattered, as a pauper. I have lost everything and every hope in life." The tears started trickling down my eyes as the sound of the lady's noises kept rising high. I soon found myself amidst a likeness of an expanse, shining brightly around me. I kept meditating on Him within that aura of peace when suddenly, something struck me deep inside that I could not discern. Although I had no visual encounter, but I felt something assuring me that I was in the presence of someone holy and divine. I kept calm and serene for some time and humbled myself in prayer to sense the sheer joy of His supernatural power around me. I could feel the gushing rivers of His love flowing through my body. I was in bliss of the whole sacred experience that kept filling me with joy and comfort. I felt God real and near than ever and wept bitterly at His feet, bursting out loud in His pure, pious presence that caught the attention of the other ladies who came to console me. Then, the leader of the group volunteered to lead me into the prayer and asked me to repeat by saying, "Jesus, I acknowledge that you are the son of God, Who died on the cross and shed your precious blood for my sins. You rose on the third day and had victory over death to give me eternal life. I am a sinner and ask you to forgive my sins. I thank you for all that you did for me. I invite you to come into my heart. I surrender my life into your hands. Be my savior. Be my King." Then, the entire group of born-again Christians presented me with a Holy Bible. I was curious to know what born-again really meant, then one of the ladies there read out the Bible scripture in John 3:3: "Jesus answered and said to him, "Most assuredly, I say to you, unless one is born again, he cannot see the kingdom of God." Then I thanked the ladies and departed from there in peace.

I started reading the Bible to know about this true living God whose presence had enamored me, and I made a goal for myself: I somehow needed to get baptized before the coming of the new millennium year of 2000 to start afresh. The Lord who knew my heart made it possible when a friend of mine invited me for a picnic arranged by the Assembly of God Church on November 29th, 1999, in Mumbai. I had no clue what the Lord had in store for me, but I joined the picnic to be close to the believers. When we reached the picnic spot, it just looked gorgeous. The cottages around the beach were all fringed with swaying palm trees. The gushing waves were roaring in a continuous pattern, crashing against the rocks at full speed and slowly subsiding as they retreated calmly. The sand looked relatively clear, and the light blue water was inviting. The spot that was booked looked serene and exclusive, away from the hustle and bustle of the rowdy groups of beachgoers. But farther away, I could see lots of families and groups. Some were running along the seaside, and some youngsters were running with their doggies and pooches. Many kids sat making houses with the sand while others were flying Frisbees. The lovers were seen seated in secluded corners, and some guys gulping beer.

No one was near our spot, which really seemed strange to me. As we settled down, I observed some ladies changing clothes and heading towards the seashore. My friend then told me that the Pastor was at the seashore waiting to baptize them and asked me if I would like to be baptized. I was pretty amazed and told her, "How can I be baptized? I was not aware of that, and I do not have another set of clothes with me." Then she opened her bag and handed me her gown. I then changed into her gown, took off my sandals, and proceeded towards the beach, holding hands. As I walked on the beach, I felt the warm, smooth sand move through my toes. I was both humbled and exuberant about the opportunity I had and felt that nature was in tune with the event. Pastor Jerry then called me first among all the ladies and ducked me down into the water to be baptized. I was ecstatic that I would now be able to make a public proclamation of my spiritual rebirth. It was a great once-in-a-lifetime experience for me to receive the Holy Spirit, and I thanked the Lord for fulfilling my heart's desire.

I realized I had ultimately found the true God, the God who loves and cares for me and with whom I can have a personal relationship. As days passed by, my passion for reading the Bible increased as it filled my empty life with words of affirmation and promises. I observed the Bible verses guiding me to obey and follow certain commandments, which revealed to me the sins I had committed through the verse in Leviticus 26:1, "You shall not make idols for yourselves; neither a carved image nor a sacred pillar shall you rear up for yourselves; nor shall you set up an engraved stone in your land, to bow down to it; for I am the LORD your GOD." My flagrant sin was clear as I had exchanged the truth for a lie. For I had been worshipping the man-made idols of wood, silver, and stone instead of the true living God, the Creator of the universe. The feeling of guilt made me repent and motivated me to get rid of all the ungodly things I had. So, I removed all the idols from the temple I had in my bedroom and images embossed in the gold and diamond jewelry that I wore.

The film production company was a major issue that bothered me the most. I had been holding all the letterheads and documents of my production company and retained the bank account in the name of goddess Kali Maa. I clearly felt the Lord wanting me to shut down the film production. It was a tough call to give away my dream. But finally, I gave in. I closed the bank account, tore off the letterheads, threw away all of the logos and stamps, destroyed all the checkbooks and documents, and closed the production company. The Sai Baba Textile Company still existed since it was my only source of income. I was in a fix and hesitant to shut it down, contending with the Lord as to how I would survive without it. How would I manage to pay my bills? His answer was clear as He spoke to me through a Bible verse, 1 Peter 5:6-7, "Therefore humble yourselves under the mighty hand of God, that He may exalt you in due time, casting all your care upon Him, for He cares for you."

I prayed and fasted, asking Him to make me self-sufficient, and waited for His answer. My loving, gracious God whispered His word to me through Matthew 6:26, "Look at the birds of the air, for they neither sow nor reap nor gather into barns; yet your heavenly Father feeds them. Are you not of more value than they?" I broke down and cried as I got my answer. I knew the Lord would provide everything for me, for He even provides for the birds that neither sow nor reap, and He definitely values me more than them. Finally, I obeyed Him to shut down the textile company, and was done with it. But the Lord was not yet done with me and had much more in store for me. It was now His time to speak into my life by proving His word to be true as a testimony for His glory.

CHAPTER 7

DREAMS THAT BLOSSOMED

Revelations Turning into Reality

The Lord then spoke into my life in His perfect time through dream revelations and transformed them into reality to manifest His Word to be true. Thus, by doing so, he not only allowed me to partake in His excellence but also gave me the privilege to share my testimonies as an example to prepare others to know the richness of His glory and power. So that we all proclaim His name and permeate the aroma of His fragrance around the nations. Isaiah 42:21 says, "The people are formed for me that they may proclaim My name." Similarly, the same Lord is always ready to speak into each one of our lives. But the question is if we are ready to listen, obey, and follow His commands. Deuteronomy 28:1 says, "If you fully obey the Lord your God and carefully follow all His commands I give you today, the Lord your God will set you high above all the nations on earth." The Bible clearly speaks that obedience to Him is the major factor for us to get us to His perfect plan of abundance. The one life we have been given to us is only one chance to have our way or to have His way for our cup to run over. Unfortunately, many miss out by not knowing what their true calling is because they do not register what the Lord has been asking and calling them to do for Him in life. He was asking mankind to surrender and to be obedient as the sheep's that follow their shepherd. God's design has always been for His anointing to come upon those whom he found were trustworthy and obedient. God tested Abraham by asking him to sacrifice his son as written in Genesis 22:2 "Take now your son, your only son Isaac, whom you love, and go to the land of Moriah, and offer him there as a burnt offering on one of the mountains of which I shall tell you."

Then Abraham obeyed the Lord and did not withhold his only son and was willing to sacrifice him when the Lord commanded him to stop and pronounced His blessings as written in Genesis 22:17 "Blessings, I will bless you, and multiplying I will multiply your descendants as the stars of heaven and as the sand which is on the seashore."

Similarly, the Lord also tested Noah as written In Genesis 6:5-6 "And God saw that the wickedness of man was great in the earth and that every imagination of the thought of his heart was only evil continually. And it repented the Lord that He had made man on the earth, and it grieved him at his heart." Then, the Lord wanted to destroy man from the face of the earth by flooding it with water. However, He wanted to save Noah, one of the eight people, a preacher of righteousness, before bringing in the flood on the world of the ungodly. So the Lord asked Noah to build an ark, and Noah obeyed and built it. Then Noah and his family entered the ark at the Lord's command. Later, when the floodgates of heaven had been closed, and the water receded steadily from the earth, Noah and his family came out of the ark that had come to rest on the mountain of Ararat, and were blessed as written in Genesis 9:1 "And God blessed Noah and his sons and said unto them, be fruitful and multiply and replenish the earth."

I knew the true living God, whom I had accepted as my Savior, was eternal and unchanging and would one day also test me. His presence in my life was so powerful that I desired to diligently obey and follow each of His commands. So, I quit singing and praising man-made idols and saints and sacrificed by giving up on all my pre-booked concert assignments. Then, I dedicated my life to Him, having a keen desire in my heart to use my vocal talent for His praise and worship. But all that was just a wishful thought of my heart. Soon, His miracle was evident when He fulfilled my desire by providing a sponsor to finance my project, and by doing so, he made my dream come true, and my first gospel album got recorded, "Yeshu tu laut ke aa," meaning, "Return O Lord."

As time passed, my relationship with the Lord grew deeper and more intense, as He heard my inner heart's voice and answered each of my desires even before I could ask for it. He dealt with me as a Father to his child and thus trained me to increase my faith. He fulfilled each of my longings, which made me believe that in Him, my thoughts are things. Gradually, my faith increased to the substance level of hope and evidence of things not seen.

It was a sad phase of my life; Mom had departed, leaving us lonely and lost. The house looked empty and soon became a silent cell of reminiscent past, reminding us each day of her loss. I was desperate to move out of the apartment, and so was my family. The property prices had skyrocketed in our area, and it was practically impossible for us to sell our old apartment and buy a new, bigger apartment. Moreover, the price difference between selling and buying another apartment was enormous, and the chances looked slim. The faithful Lord moved again, for nothing is ever impossible in His kingdom, and He made it possible for us to get a bigger three-bedroom apartment in a brand-new building in Bandra for the same price that we sold our two-bedroom Bandra apartment in the previous building.

Things changed drastically before I could move to the new apartment. The Bible verse of His promise assured me as written in 1 Peter 5:10 "But the God of all grace, who hath called us unto His eternal glory by

Christ Jesus, after that ye have suffered a while, make you perfect, establish, strengthen, settle you." Since I had not completed reading the whole Bible, my knowledge of the word was limited, but the power of the verses that I called to mind was daily gaining prominence in my life as they kept transforming into reality. I could clearly see the Lord in my life. Things started changing, and so did my attitude. I saw myself drifting away from television and soap operas, which were my priorities before I accepted the Lord. The Holy Spirit, my comforter and counselor, kept guiding and leading me and oftentimes convicted me at night to be in the presence of the Lord, where sometimes, out of love, I thanked Him and at other times would cry for mercy. My personal experience with the Lord each day kept on increasing my faith to make me understand how I need to respond to His commands.

It was one of those lonely nights when I had a dream. I saw myself standing on the 100th floor of one of the two tall buildings and observed a huge crane moving up and down, picking up the debris. On the crane sat a young girl, cross-legged like a seesaw, holding a little baby to have fun. I was petrified and started shouting, but no one could hear my voice due to the thick, closed glass windows on the high tower and amidst the sound of a plane flying across the sky. I wanted the crane to stop moving so that I could save the girl and the baby. I could not figure out what the dream really meant, but being moved by it and remembering every intricate detail of it, I painted it on a sheet. Then, I took it to share it with my pastor in the church, who had often spoken about the Lord and His ability to communicate with us through His Word, dreams, and visions. Then, the lady in the church who observed my painting interpreted it and said, "The two tall buildings are the Twin Towers in New York, and each has a hundred floors. The crane lifting the girl is the sign of you being lifted up, and the plane signifies your journey to America." Trusting that the Lord had spoken to me through my dream, I started praying to Him to turn my dream into reality.

A few months later, I was booked for a concert in Hong Kong. I was ecstatic to perform once again after a long lapse of time. The trip turned out to be great as more and more bookings came in due to the success of my first show. The payments were huge, and I had received Hong Kong currency, but I exchanged them for U.S. dollars, being led by the spirit. Then I realized maybe it was the Lord's provision for my trip, but I still had doubts that maybe it was a coincidence. Then I asked Him to provide me with the airplane ticket, and I felt that would be really tough for Him! How will He be able to send me that by post? But His thoughts are different than our thoughts, and His ways are different than our ways. So it all happened when a friend of mine visited me after I had returned from Hong Kong, complaining that I could have taken her along with me since I had a complimentary hotel room with meals. Then I told her, "So true, it never occurred to me, but you can join me for my next concert trip." On her second visit to my place, she said, "I might get some complimentary tickets, then you can join me." I said, "Okay, we can do that." Later, she left, and I soon forgot all about it. I was waiting and testing my Lord's ability. Then, out of the blue, she called up and said, "I got the two tickets, and my husband said free tickets mean nothing. You still have to pay for hotels, food, and conveyance; trips are not cheap; they are really expensive to fly to America, so I don't think we can go." When she said America, I was dazed and told her that I could go all by myself if God wished. Time passed by and later I found an envelope under my door and when I opened it, I saw an open buddy Delta Airlines ticket to America. My limited knowledge of His revelation turning into reality put me in utter shame for testing the Lord. I was extremely grateful that He provided me with the ticket, but I was still nervous about traveling alone. I had no contacts in America and had no idea what I would be doing there. So, by faith, I packed my suitcase with hundreds of CDs of my album that were recorded by His grace. His voice about the trip was loud and clear in my spirit; though I didn't hear His audible voice, I wrestled within myself out of fear and insecurity. But His continuous guidance and provision made it emphatically clear to me that it was His plan. Then, I no longer hesitated or doubted. I walked upright in faith and responded the way Isaiah did, "Here I am, Lord. Send me!" Trusting Him, I walked into the airline office to redeem my Delta voucher and booked the flight. The lady at the desk asked me for details about the two free stops I was entitled to take. I was blank and had no idea where I was supposed to go. I waited for a while and later found the spirit nudging me to go to San Francisco. The ticket I booked was from Mumbai to New York, then San Francisco, and then to New York, and a return back to Mumbai. I had packed my bags and had two days left before boarding the flight. I knew nothing about America and wondered where I would stay and what I would do. Late that evening, I received a call from my pastor inviting me home to have a cup of coffee with him. Though I hesitated a lot, I decided to go. Then I shared with him about the Lord's provision and His faithfulness by turning my dream revelation into reality. I even told him that I was still not sure what the Lord's plan was and how He would use me in New York. He then prayed with me and asked me to trust the Lord, for He is sufficient to make a way for you. So, after praying for a while and having coffee with him, I returned home and retired to bed.

Soon, the day of my departure arrived, and I reached the airport and waited in line for the immigration formalities to be completed. After a long wait, the Delta crew announced that the flight was full and requested the buddy ticket travelers not to wait any longer. Then I left my luggage at the Mumbai airport locker and returned home disappointed, not knowing what was next in store for me. A few days later, I inquired at the Delta office about the next possible opening for the buddy ticket holders to travel, and I got confirmation to report for the next day's flight.

Early in the morning of the next day, while I was still in bed, I received a call from a gentleman from New York who had been trying to contact me for a while. He told me that he got the news about my visit to New York from his friend. He told me how much he had enjoyed my concert in Pune, India, and had been keen on making videos of my songs for his gospel TV channel in New York. He asked if I would be kind enough to accommodate him by making my shoot dates available to him. He also requested that it would be his privilege if I agreed to be his guest. I then gave him my shoot dates and arrival details, and he said he would be honored to meet me at the airport.

After I hung up, I knelt down and cried out, thanking the Lord for His love and care. I spoke with Him for a long time, praising Him and thanking Him for the peace and joy I now have about this trip. That evening, I was back at the airport, waiting in the long line for my turn at the counter. Suddenly, one of the airline officers called me up front and said the flight was full, and they had no seats available, but they would upgrade me to first class. I was flabbergasted as to why they would upgrade me among so many other passengers who had already been waiting ahead of me. The airline officer then took my buddy's ticket and gave me the boarding pass for first class.

All through my flight, I kept thinking about how the Lord's network works. He used the pastor to send the email to his friend in New York. He delayed my trip to a later date so that the gentleman from New York could contact and host me. Plus, he arranged for me to travel by first class and my gospel songs telecasted on the Gospel TV channel for His glory. My heart was humbled with gratitude as I experienced Him moving mightily in my life.

After reaching New York and completing the video shoots, everything just accelerated. The videos were released on the New York TV channel and touched the hearts of thousands. My first concert in the U.S. was arranged by a church in Flushing, New York. The success of that concert spread like wildfire. Many concert bookings were quickly made without me contacting anyone or having an agent work for me. Many pastors received calls from other pastors in different cities wanting to invite me to perform in their churches. They worked out among themselves all the details of my itinerary, my tickets, my hotel accommodations, and the love offering.

I only received an e-ticket number to board the flight and was given the name of the pastor who would host and receive me.

I was booked to perform all over America with concerts arranged in different denominational churches all across New Jersey, New York, Chicago, Atlanta, Portland, San Francisco, Dallas, Houston, Washington, D.C., South Carolina, Maryland, and St. Augustine, Florida.

I flew back and forth tirelessly for six months and performed in numerous churches and stadiums. I was in a state of bliss, having the privilege of glorifying my Lord by sharing my testimony on every stage and pulpit. I walked in faith, obeying the Lord. I never felt concerned or ever thought of what I would do if no one arrived at the airport to receive me. I carried no cell phone or laptop with me, nor did I make any prior hotel bookings. The Lord was my all in all.

Finally, the Lord's six-month assignment till my visa expiry was accomplished, and I was now set to return home to Mumbai. That night, I started wondering about my new apartment. My family had already taken possession of it, but I had no idea what the decor was like or which bedroom I would have for myself. The master bedroom was really lavish, and I thought since I was the eldest, I would get first priority in selecting a bedroom.

That night, before leaving for India, I had a dream. I observed myself traveling in a chauffeur-driven car. I was seated in the center of the backseat with both my sisters on either side of me. As the car reached the highway, it stopped suddenly, blocked by a traffic jam. I was frustrated and then observed myself standing out of the car and viewing hundreds of cars being stranded bumper to bumper. Suddenly, I was lifted up in the air and gone. When I woke up the next morning, I remembered my dream but could not figure out what it meant. I was in a hurry to pack my bags as it was time for me to leave for the airport to board the flight back to Mumbai.

When I reached Mumbai, I was thrilled to see my new apartment. When I entered it, I felt so blessed. It looked just great, but the final colors of the three bedrooms were not yet done due to my absence. Now that I had returned, it was time to decide which room and color each one desired. My sisters suggested that we cast lots. It was at that moment the Lord told me, "You shall not stay here, for I will lift you up. Let your sisters choose the room they desire, and you shall take what is left." Then, I clearly understood what the car dream meant. I suggested that they take their choice of rooms without casting lots. Then, they both chose the rooms on either side of the apartment, exactly as they were seated in the car, and the center room was left for me. It was exactly as the Lord had shown to me through the dream. I then took the center room, painted it, and decorated it the way I wanted. The lovely view of the lighted cross above the church from my bedroom windows each day reminded me of my Lord watching over me and His faithfulness to lead me to a place of promise in the new home that He had provided for me.

Not only did the Lord settle me into my new apartment, but He made me walk through every difficult situation in my life with the knowledge that He was beside me. Zee TV, one of the most popular channels in India, offered to promote me and signed me as their contractual artist for five years, which opened a new door for me to gain a name and fame in the commercial field. The contract was to record, shoot, and telecast my songs on their TV channel, to book me for live concerts, and to promote me all across the nation. I was ecstatic to get such a great break and was all set to go ahead. On one of my visits to the Zee office, I was informed about the strategy they had planned to launch for me. Their initial choice was to release the most prestigious album that I had recorded with Anup Jalota, a top-notch singer from India. I agreed with their choice, and they asked me if I could arrange with Anup Jalota about the availability of his dates for shooting the video. I wasn't really pleased about all this, but I still went ahead and discussed it with Anup Jalota and gave them the shoot dates. Their plan was to shoot it in Shirdi, where the Sai Baba temple is located. They took our dates three times and failed to get permission from the temple authorities due to the outpouring rush of thousands of people who thronged each day to pay homage to the temple. In the meantime, Zee planned all the publicity and printed the fliers. I was nervous and uncomfortable about it and felt in my spirit that I was stuck in a rut. I realized the sin I was about to commit by singing praises and glorifying a Hindu saint on the TV channel. I knew it was Satan's plan to lure me once again into his grip by enticing me with worldly gains, and it was not the Lord who had blessed me. I asked for forgiveness and prayed to the Lord to get me out of the contract deal. I knew my Lord was in control since He had deprived the Zee company of obtaining permission for the shooting three different times at the temple. Knowing the truth and being convinced by the Holy Spirit, I burned all the publicity fliers that I had on the terrace of my building that were to be pasted all over the streets in Mumbai. The Lord later helped to get me released from the Zee contract without any hassle and blessed me to only serve Him.

The Lord always stood by His promise that He would never leave me nor forsake me. On one of my return trips back home to Mumbai, I was encouraged by a realtor to invest in property since the buzz was that property prices in Mumbai were still going to skyrocket. There were lots of realtors who took me around to see different properties on sale. After a long search, I decided to buy a small apartment close to the beach, as suggested by a lady realtor. The view was lovely, and I loved the surroundings. The next day,

I paid the deposit of thirty-five thousand rupees to the owner and finalized the deal. That night, the Lord spoke to me through another dream. I saw myself standing on a high mountain and the lady realtor standing next to me. All of a sudden, I saw her pushing me down from the mountain. I saw myself falling down and screaming loudly, which woke me up with a start. The next morning, I realized that the Lord had informed me that the realtor had tricked me into falling for this deal and that I had committed a blunder. I knew if I canceled the deal, my deposit would be forfeited. So, I scrambled around town to procure property documents from the municipality and other sources to learn more about the land and details of the apartment I had bought. I learned that the lease on the land had expired, and I would not own the land under my small apartment. Plus, the landowners had full rights to demolish any unauthorized construction on their land. I thanked the Lord for speaking to me in my dream and cried out to Him to help me get my deposit back. The next day, I met the owners of the property to whom I was supposed to pay the remaining full and final amount. Instead, I asked them for my deposit back and told them I was not interested in going ahead with the deal. The Lord somehow changed their hearts, and they unexpectedly returned my entire deposit with no penalty.

Since then, I have been receptive to the Lord and have kept my spiritual ears open to hear the inner voice, as I am no more attuned to the sounds and noises of this world. I had vividly learned how to participate with God and to be obedient to move ahead according to His plan and purpose in my life.

I believe that when you take one humble step in obedience, God will lead and guide you toward the next step. The Lord gave me the task of making more music for Him, and I started working on the lyrics and composing music. Finally, I recorded two more albums in Hindi, "Mujhe Maaf Karna," meaning "Forgive me, Lord," and another, "Dil Se," meaning "With love." For the Lord knew I would need more praise and worship songs to glorify Him. I was prepared and set to go wherever He desired, but my heart's desire was to go to America to witness the historic 2000 New Year's Millennium celebration ball at Times Square, New York. I thought the only way possible for me to witness this spectacular event was if someone booked me for the concert.

So, knowing the inner desire of my heart, the Lord did the needful and made it possible for me to be in America, as I was invited to perform by the Federation of Indo-American Christians Association on December 8, 2000, in Chicago. I was very excited to be there, and the concert went well. But what surprised me the most was when I was called upon the stage for the second time to receive a Lifetime Achievement Millennium Award for my abiding commitment to preaching the Word of God through music to the nations. I was in awe and extremely humbled. The Lord blessed me in double measure, for not only did He give me a chance to be in the U.S. to witness this historic Millennium celebration, but He also allowed me to be honored with the Millennium Award. There were times when I wondered how the omnipotent God who created the universe still cared for me to hear and answer each and every desire of my heart.

He never stopped and kept opening more doors. One day, I received a call from Mr. Jay, a church elder in New York, asking me about my availability to perform at the Revival Crusade and Music Fest that he was organizing in New York City. He asked me if I would be available to share the platform with the renowned revival speaker, Rev. Samuel Rodrigues, from California. After booking the venue at the Martin Van Buren High School in Queens, New York, and scheduling the final dates, Mr. Jay requested me to book my round-trip ticket from Mumbai to New York, promising that he would reimburse the amount to me as soon as I reach New York.

I then booked my ticket and arrived in New York. The revival crusade was powerful, and the auditorium was jam-packed. The concert was a huge success and appreciated by all. After a few days, Mr. Jay invited me for a meal at his residence and informed me that he had to leave for India to attend a wedding. He said his brother had lined up other concerts for me in Dallas, and he would be hosting me. I was surprised that he was leaving without reimbursing me the airfare of sixty-two thousand rupees ($1300) or even a customary love offering that churches routinely observe.

Later, I left for Dallas to be hosted by Mr. Jay's brother. He had planned a huge concert there, where he and the other local artists were to share the stage with me. After my concert the local artists took over, so lots of people came to congratulate me, behind the stage and among them was a man named Mr. Johnson and his wife who chatted with me for a while and then invited me for supper at their residence for the next day. So, I accepted their invitation. Then the concert ended, and Mr. Jay's brother, my host, drove us back to his home. During supper, he informed me that he and his wife had plans to leave for India for the wedding as well and suggested that he would appreciate it if I could make my own arrangement to stay in a hotel by tomorrow.

Then I packed my suitcase before I retired to bed and cried out to the Lord to help me. I was troubled as they failed to keep their word to reimburse my ticket amount. Somehow, late after prayer and petition in my bed, I dozed off to sleep. That night, I had a dream, and I saw myself walking in a garden full of colorful flowers. Far ahead, I saw a typical ancient mansion covered with ivy hanging all over the structure and its walls. Its huge front door was surrounded by creeping vines and shrubs. As I moved closer, I saw the front door open and a man in a long, white gown walk towards me. He had a key in his hand and He handed it to me, and disappeared. Early the next morning, I shared the dream with the wife of my host that the Lord had provided a key to me, but I could not discern what it meant. Late that evening, my host returned from his work and drove me off to Johnson's residence, where I had been invited for supper. When I got there, Johnson told me about their own ministry and how he and his wife had been serving the Lord with their musical talents. As we conversed through the evening, they expressed their desire to me and said, "We are very keen that you stay with us and bless this house." After supper, they showed me around their new palatial house, brought me to the guest room, and said, "This is your room. No one has ever slept on this bed." The guest room was new, spacious, and lovely, but I hesitated to accept their offer. Then, after much persuasion, I finally agreed. Johnson volunteered to drive me back to my host's home, but the Lord turned things around. Instead, I went to my host's house and picked up my suitcase, leaving a message with the host's kids that I was departing. Then, I drove back with Johnson to his place and slept in peace in the newly decorated bedroom that the Lord provided for me. The next day, early in the morning, before leaving for their jobs, the Johnsons brought in the key of their house and gave it to me, saying, "You have the freedom to go out and come in at your leisure." After they left, I was dumbfounded as

I held the key in my hand and was amazed by the Lord's love for turning my dream revelation into reality.

The real experience of each dream made me rejoice about the deep, intimate relationship that I shared with my Lord. It was too precious, as He made me complete in Him. I could not ask for anything more. The Lord later used me and the Johnsons to glorify Him in Dallas. There were lots of concerts lined up as the Lord kept on opening new doors for months.

Later on, I left for Atlanta as I had been invited by the First Baptist Church there. My host was Sushma, a church member who was married to a German man. They had a lovely three-story bungalow on top of a hill. They stayed on the second floor, and I had the entire first floor at my disposal. The view from their house was just amazing. The only time we met was during supper, as Sushma left early in the morning for her job. I had two concerts scheduled there and was to stay with them for five days. The first concert was held at the First Baptist Church, which went off well and was a huge success. Soon, more bookings came in, and I had to extend my stay there. My toiletries, soap, and toothpaste were all used up. I needed to buy more. I felt embarrassed to ask for these tiny favors from my host.

I was in a dilemma and needed someone to drive me to the store. It was exactly at that moment that Pastor Farhat of the Asian church called me up, informing me that Mr. Bob had invited me for lunch, and he was coming to fetch me. He then told me that Mr. Bob Franklin was the director of the North American World Mission, who had attended and liked my concert at his church. I was glad to hear that and thought to myself that now I would be able to buy my toiletries. The pastor came very late to fetch me as one of his church members had expired that day. He was upset as he was already late for the luncheon meeting. I asked him if he could take me to the mall, and he said he would do it after lunch.

The meeting with Bob went well, and after we finished lunch, the pastor kept getting calls to pick up the children from the school of the church member who had expired that morning. We then thanked Bob for the delicious meal and walked out. When we reached the corridor, a lady stopped us at the entrance of a huge hall and handed a brochure to us, insisting we visit the exhibition in the hall. The pastor was busy on the phone, confused and in a rush, and was now reluctant to take me to the mall or to take time for the exhibit. While he was busy on his cell phone making arrangements to pick up the children, the lady took me into the hall. As I walked around looking at the things displayed at the exhibit, I was astonished to see two huge tables, one loaded with mini soaps and the other with mini-Colgate toothpaste. The lady escorting me asked if I would like to have some samples, and I joyfully said yes. I could not believe that the Lord loved me so much and provided every small need I had. The pastor was amazed as I walked out with my brand of toothpaste and soap in my hand. After that, I carried the samples to every stage where I performed just to testify and glorify Jesus and the intimacy I shared with Him.

During that period, a gentleman known as Brother George was on a mission to reach out to the unbelievers in Portland, Oregon. He had been praying to the Lord to open the doors for him. Somehow, he had heard about my ministry and booked me for a concert, and after my confirmation, he sent all the fliers and invitations to all the other churches in his vicinity. When I arrived in Portland, Brother George was very nervous. He told me about the phone calls he had received from local Hindus asking about the style of music I would be singing. Most of them, after observing the fliers, thought I would sing Bollywood film songs. Brother George told them they would know more about my music if they attended the concert. The next day, when I reached the auditorium, it was jam-packed. Brother George and many of his church members were nervous, but I was full of spirit and walked onto the stage with confidence. I observed all the Hindus seated and felt comfortable communicating with them since I was a former Hindu.

After being introduced on stage, I started my concert, and after my first song, I heard the thundering sound of applause. I then shared my testimony, sang another song, and continued the pattern, sharing how the Lord has been moving in my life. The audience sat quietly and dumbfounded as they listened to my testimonies. Soon, the concert ended, and the audience lined up to greet me and thanked me for sharing my testimonies. It was the happiest moment of my life and Brother George's life to succeed in this mission of bringing the gospel to Hindus. I knew in my spirit that I had sown the seeds in Portland, which the Lord, in due course of time, would allow it to flourish.

The Lord provided opportunities for me to reach out to people of different castes, creeds, and religions. I was invited to a convention in Singapore to reach out to the Sindhi community, a group from Pakistan. I felt a need to record albums in Sindhi, so I went ahead and recorded two Sindhi albums. The concert turned out to be a blessing, and I had the privilege of touching the hearts of many Sindhis. After departing from Singapore, I was booked to perform in Malaysia, a Muslim country. The Malaysian organizers there were a bit concerned that glorifying Jesus might create some trouble with the Muslims. I, on the other hand, trusted the Lord and thanked Him for opening the door to spread the gospel there. The concert was a great success as the Lord had allowed us to sow many more seeds.

Pakistan was another Muslim country where some recording companies had duplicated my CDs to sell them.

Though I could have sued them under the copyright law, I preferred not to, as I felt my mission to spread the gospel was being accomplished. My songs became very popular in Pakistan, and then Pastor Gill invited me to perform in Lahore at the Word of Life Crusade, which was to be held at the Gaddafi Stadium in Pakistan. The situation there was bad due to the assassination of a political leader, and there were lots of riots. I was still keen on going, but the Lord intervened, and I was detained by the immigration authorities. I had lots of other invitations to perform in Pakistan, but I had an Indian passport, and I was unable to obtain a visa each time I tried to visit Pakistan.

Europe was another place where I was invited by Prophet Dr. Owuor from Kenya to join him for The International Conference in Amsterdam, hosted in collaboration with all the revival churches of the Netherlands, Europe, Africa, Canada, and the United States. The fliers were printed, and all the publicity was done. On the departure date, I arrived at the airport and checked in my luggage but was unable to board the flight as I had no visa for Amsterdam, only a green card. Though I was disappointed and missed the opportunity to glorify God, I still knew He had better plans in store.

Each day brought new surprises and blessings for me. The Lord led me to meet specific people who made suggestions about His plan for my life. I wanted to relax and take a short trip, and a friend of mine suggested that

I take a holiday trip to visit her in Australia. I wondered what I would do in Australia and prayed to the Lord, asking Him to reveal the plan He had for me. My agreement with the Lord was that if my friend called me and again insisted I come to Australia, I would know it was His plan. Within a week, I got a call from my friend asking me about my arrival date. I knew the Lord had answered my prayer but still had no idea how He would use me there. I went ahead and booked my ticket in faith and informed my friend about my arrival. She was thrilled and said her brother would meet me at the Sydney airport, and later, she and her other family members would meet us at a restaurant for supper. On my arrival in Australia, her brother and his son received me at the airport and then took me to their residence. After I rested and freshened up, we left to join his other family members at an Italian restaurant. Late that night, when I retired to bed, I was uncomfortable and felt deceived because I was not hosted by my friend but rather by her brother, with whom I felt she was probably trying to fix me up. I was hurt and prayed to the Lord to take me out of this rut that I was in and to relocate me to a place where He could use me.

When I awoke early in the morning, I found the house empty, and my breakfast lay on the table. As I was having my breakfast in the empty house, the spirit clearly told me to pick up the telephone directory and call. I was confused and could not understand why and whom to call, and what to say. Being obedient, I followed the command, remembering an old saying that "the thought you never think is from God, and godly thought is from God." I opened the directory and started browsing through the pages of names and numbers of the long list of churches and pastors. I searched for a long time until finally, my eyes became fixed on a certain particular number. The spirit clearly nudged me and said to call that pastor's number. All this may sound really foolish to non-believers, thinking who could be so stupid as to go to a different country and pick up the huge directory to call some unknown strangers and expect to get a response? But as a strong believer, I knew that the Lord works in mysterious ways, for He chose the foolish things of the world to confound the wise and the weak things of the world to confound the mighty. For example, the Lord wanted Joshua to gain victory and capture Jericho. The walls of Jericho were very strong, and no one could enter the city. The Lord told Joshua to circle around the walls seven times and then shout loudly to enter the city. He obeyed the Lord and walked around the walls seven times, and the strong walls came crashing down. Joshua and his army entered the city, killed all the inhabitants, and got the victory by capturing Jericho. I knew my Lord was leading me the same way.

Then I picked up the phone and dialed that number but got no response, so I left a message for the pastor instead. After a while, Pastor George returned the call, and I introduced myself to him. He was exceedingly pleased to meet me and invited me to join him for the prayer meeting and supper that he had arranged that evening. I then thanked him for the honor of inviting me and told him that I didn't have a ride. He said, "I will ask the pastor in your vicinity to come and fetch you. You just give me your address." I had no address, so I picked up the post that was lying on the dining table of my host and read the address to him. He said, "Hope to see you soon. May the Lord bless you." After he hung up, I was elated and felt blessed to join a new bunch of pastors and believers in Australia. Later, by evening, the pastor and his wife arrived to fetch me, and then they invited my hosts also to join us for supper, but they refused the invitation. Then we left and chatted all through the drive, and the pastor later registered that he had heard a lot about my ministry and was pleased to meet me in person. When we reached the conference room, Pastor George introduced me to all the committee members. Later, they asked me to sing for them. After I sang, things just changed. All the CDs that I had carried were soon sold out, and all those who heard me complimented me and asked for my cell number. I explained to them that I had arrived yesterday and had no cell number yet. Pastor George then announced that I was his guest and they could contact me for any bookings on his cell phone.

Later, we had supper and left to drive back home. As we drove, Pastor George thought the trip was time-consuming and long and suggested it would be better if I had stayed close to his church. He then asked me if it was okay for me to stay with a lady member of his church to make it easy for him to reach me rather than staying so far off with the non-believers. I was absolutely amazed by his proposal and realized the Lord had sent the pastor to make arrangements for me to shift elsewhere. I agreed with the pastor and decided to move out. When we reached home, I packed my bags and said adieu to my friend's brother and son, thanking them for their hospitality, and then I left with the pastor to stay with his lady church member. When I retired to bed that night in my lovely new house, I humbled myself in prayer to thank God for His instant favor of relocating me immediately.

My heart was filled with extreme gratitude for the relationship I shared with my Lord. I knew the Lord had orchestrated things to bring the new pastor into my life to fulfill His plan to use me for His glory. His new plan for me to minister started when the Victory Mission Church arranged my first concert to reach out to the people in Australia. The Lord's mercy was enormous, and the concert was a huge success. There was no turning back as more pastors from various churches arranged additional concerts.

During that period, the family of Dhinakaran arrived to inaugurate their prayer tower, and all the churches were excited to attend "Jesus Calls Australia Power Ministry." It was to be conducted by Evangelical preacher Dr. D.G.S. Dhinakaran, who drew thousands, where many were experiencing miraculous healing. During that meeting, I was amazed when his son, Evangelist Dr. Paul Dhinakaran, walked up to me and complimented me on my CD, which he had already heard that morning, and asked if it was possible for me to join their ministry and perform at their meetings. I thanked him and said I would be honored to do so. My gracious Lord fulfilled the deep desire that I had yearned for to serve Him and allowed me to be in a position with the Dhinakarans to minister through my music to thousands in Australia. When the heart of a man cooperates with the heart of God, all things become possible. Whatever is done at His command is accomplished by His strength.

Knowing and serving God taught me a lot about the characteristics of God. As a former Hindu, I had never known why God created us and what His plan and purpose were for our lives. Accepting Jesus as my Savior was a revolutionary experience that restructured my goals in life. It not only changed my priorities in life but also taught me how to serve, love, and be humble as He humbled Himself and washed the feet of His disciples. He left His kingdom to suffer for our sins, for He loved the world so much. He shed His blood to cleanse us of all our sins, to present us before the Father as His first fruits of righteousness so that we will have eternal life with Him. The Lord made it so simple for man to be with Him in heaven if we only opened our spiritual eyes to see, hear, obey, and follow Him. Satan comes to rob, steal, and destroy us, but the Bible has given us all the tools to fight the powers and principalities of darkness.

There are no words in the dictionary sufficient to thank the Lord and no words of gratitude that can relay all He did for all of mankind and for me. My life may not be perfect, but I am surely blessed in Him.

His blessings never stopped in my life. Soon, I was booked to perform at concerts all over New Zealand and Australia. I was excited and asked my sister to join me on this trip. The first miracle of the Lord she witnessed was at one of my concerts in Sydney. On the day of my concert, early in the morning, I was unable to speak to her and lost my voice completely. The concert that was organized in a huge auditorium had been completely sold out. The noted singer Esther King was booked to share the stage with me. I cried to the Lord, asking Him to help me and not put me to shame. I walked on stage by His power, trusting that He would sing for me. My sister was very nervous but absolutely flabbergasted as soon as I opened my mouth to sing. The Lord was faithful, and His power was evident in my praises as I regained my voice and sang with a passionate heart, glorifying Him. It was by His grace, one of my best performances that touched the hearts of many.

There were many more concerts lined up for me in Melbourne and Sydney before I left for New Zealand. The Lord later blessed me as I ministered all over New Zealand and performed in Wellington, Hamilton, Palmerston, North Island, Rotorua, Auckland, Tauranga, and New Plymouth. Traveling around New Zealand and reaching the unreached was such a great joy.

Doing concerts and traveling often to distant lands was very exhausting, demanding, and challenging for me. Getting in and out of planes, changing terminals, and waiting long hours to board connecting flights sometimes took its toll on me. My vocal cords would sometimes get affected, especially when there were climatic changes from cold to hot or vice versa.

Then, back in India, I was booked for an open healing crusade to be held in Goa, where it was difficult to minister because of the opposition from the Catholic churches. After much prayer, permission was obtained to have the open-air meetings. Hundreds of people were to attend that meeting and were looking forward to being healed and blessed. Different groups and ministries joined together to arrange for this event. The Gideons volunteered to present free Bibles, and others supplied snacks and water bottles. I was to perform at that healing crusade, but I had another concert in Mumbai prior to that. My concert that night ended late, and I had to rush straight to the airport to board my flight to Goa. When I reached Goa in the morning, I had lost my voice and could hardly speak. My vocal cords had been strained at the previous night's concert because I had to sing loudly without a microphone. I was very nervous and prayed and prayed fervently to the Lord to heal me. Trusting and relying on the Lord that He would not cause me to fail, late that evening, I walked on the open stage to be introduced by the organizers. I started to perform, and as soon as I opened my mouth, I was amazed to hear my voice transform into a flowing, melodious, silky sound. I knew it was not me but the sign and wonder of the Lord. The preachers who were to conduct the healing after my performance stood dumbfounded and motioned for me to continue performing. Upon their instructions, I performed twice as long as I had been scheduled. During the concert, I shared my testimony of receiving the healing by His power to be able to sing that night. The Catholic Church leaders who knew that I had been unable to speak during the day were amazed when they witnessed the power of the spirit working in me. The whole episode turned out to be a blessing in disguise. Later, the Lord opened their church doors for me to minister and glorify Him in all the Catholic churches in Goa.

The gracious Lord also opened the door for me when Life Bread International invited me to minister in the Fiji Islands and Australia. The journey was very tedious. I had to fly from America to Mumbai, then from Mumbai to Brisbane, and then from Brisbane to Nadi, Fiji. The time period was limited, and the mission was to reach out to the maximum number of people. There were a total number of nineteen concerts scheduled for me in Fiji and Australia. The first concert was at Lautoka the day after my arrival, which went well, and I had three concerts lined up for the next day. Early the next morning, I felt feverish, my body ached, and I felt extremely weak, doubting that I would not be able to perform. But again, by His grace, I was able to perform well, and the three concerts were highly appreciated. Late that night, in my hotel room, I developed a high fever and started shivering and then continued to feel worse. A doctor was called in by the hotel staff, who suggested I rest completely and should not strain myself by doing any more concerts. I was extremely heartbroken and was not ready to give up and let go of my passion to serve God. I knew it was Satan's plan to hinder me. Fiji is a place where people practice black magic, worship idols, and call on the dead spirits, so I felt that God had led me to minister there to bring light into the darkness and to witness to these people the true living God.

My mission there was to preach the gospel and portray the love of Jesus to the lost. By the power of His grace,

I went ahead the next day and did the fifth concert. As long as I stood on the stage and sang His praises, His mercy was evident. I gained His strength, and my voice sounded perfect and melodious. But when I left the stage, I felt sick and weak inside again. The medications prescribed by the doctor were ineffective, and the fever escalated. Soon, I developed acidity and hypothyroidism. Somehow, I continued the ministry work and completed three more concerts, simultaneously running in and out of clinics and being put on IV drips. Later, I was unable to swallow food or liquids and was completely dehydrated. Many churches and believers in Fiji were praying for my healing when it was announced that my condition was serious. I had no strength and was unable to do even my personal chores. Pastor Ray's wife, Nadira, was a God-sent angel who helped me take my medications, fed me, walked me to the bathroom, and even helped me get dressed.

After having completed eight concerts in Lautoka, I had to travel to Navua. I had no energy to board the flight, so instead, the pastor and his wife drove me by car. My condition worsened on the way. We checked into the Coral Resort, where they called for a nurse to put me on an IV drip. I could hardly stand or walk and was in bad shape. The almighty God of the universe who knew my heart and my passion to serve Him became my strength, and by His power, I was able to perform five more concerts at Navua, Nasinu, Peace Chapel, Bethany Church, and

Nakasi. After having performed thirteen concerts, my condition worsened further due to gastroenteritis, and I was admitted to the hospital. No matter how much Satan tried to stop me from ministering, one thing I was sure of that is written in 1 John 4:4 "Ye are of God, little children, and have overcome them; because greater is He that is in you, than he who is in the world."

I knew my Lord is greater and would lift me out of bed to finish my mission in Fiji and help me perform the last two concerts scheduled at the Dudley Methodist Church and at the Dudley Ladies Fellowship.

The next day at the Dudley Methodist Church, I had no clue as to how I was able to stand for an hour and a half at a stretch and perform the entire concert. Only my Lord can explain how I succeeded. That night after the concert, I was miserable, running in and out of the restroom, feeling nauseated and vomiting. I was scheduled to leave Fiji the next evening and had to pack my things, but I had no plastic bags, so I wrapped my slippers in toilet paper. I heard someone say, "This is exactly how I will embalm you." I assured myself that this could not be the Lord speaking but rather the wicked one, Satan. I was shivering and could hardly stand. I was sure I would die. But I somehow managed to walk out of the bathroom and collapsed on my bed, crying out to the Lord to heal me. I was alone in Fiji and knew if I died, there would be no one to bury me in this distant land. I fell on my knees, pleading to the Lord to come and heal me, and said, "Lord, if only I could touch the hem of your garment, I know I will be healed." I prayed and prayed, calling on Him earnestly and pleading, "If you are the true God, reveal yourself to me and heal me." Then my Lord, my God, reminded me of Luke 10:19 "Behold, I give you the authority to trample on serpents and scorpions, and over all the power of the enemy, and nothing shall by any means hurt you."

His comforting words were like a soothing balm to me, but still, I was restless, calling Him to come and heal me. I prayed and pleaded until, finally, I dozed off. I had a dream and saw myself lying on the bed. Suddenly, someone clasped me tightly in his arms from behind me and pulled me close to his body. I could hardly move my head to see who it was, but I was appalled when I saw his black, hairy, huge hands holding me, which took the breath out of me. He kept pressing me tighter in his grip as if choking me. I tried to move and scream but was unable to do so. I struggled for a long time, fighting and rebuking him, calling on the name of the Lord until he finally let me loose and was gone. I got up with a jerk and checked my bedroom door and windows to see if anyone had entered my room, but everything was locked. I knew Satan had come in disguise to attack me, so I covered myself with the precious blood of Jesus and put on the armor of the Lord. I kept praying and praying fervently to the Lord again and again, "If you are a true God, you will come and heal me. Let this sickness and trials of mine be all to Your glory." I kept repeating the prayers until I was lost in another dream, where I saw a man seated on the bench in my bedroom. He had a book in his hand and was reading. I then went and sat on the other end of his bench. He looked and smiled at me. I gave him a second glance, and then I went still closer to him, caught his face in both of my hands and said, "I know You are Jesus. I know you are, aren't You?" Suddenly, he rose and appeared in his true form, revealing himself to me. His white satin robe had full, long-flowing sleeves, and he stood tall above the ground. There was the feeling of electricity in his body, and his sleeves were enlarged as if filled with a whirlwind. I was dazed as he hovered over me. I caught hold of his garment and said, "Lord, I won't let go of you. You are true and Holy. You heard my cry and came. Now don't leave me, Lord, don't leave me." I tried to grasp the hem of his garment as tight as I could, but He soon disappeared.

The unforeseen meeting and the glimpse of the spiritual encounter with the Lord overwhelmed me with His glory and holiness. I got out of my bed in a state of awe and shouted, "Lord, you are a true God! Lord, you are a true God! I know. You heard me and came! Blessed am I to be in your presence!" I realized the Lord had spiritually prepared me to go through this encounter with Him. For not only did He display His glory and excellence to me, but he also blessed me to partake of His grace and radiance.

I thanked Him and kept praising Him till it was early morning. I was still in a state of awe and wonder and was eager to share my encounter with His Majesty. I had my concert scheduled at the Dudley Ladies Fellowship in Suva, and I felt I had regained enough strength that morning, as I was able to do all my chores. Then, before I could leave, I swallowed my food for the first time in days and enjoyed my breakfast.

I felt healthy and exuberant when I walked up to the stage. Then, I attended the whole concert, singing praises to the Lord and sharing my testimony of the healing that I had received personally from Him. The concert was then over, and my pastor and his wife drove me to the hospital for my final checkups and tests. The senior doctor who brought in my test reports surprised me when he informed me that the report was good and I was absolutely fit to travel. After thanking him, I left for Naya Jiwan Radio Station, where I was scheduled for my interview. Then, during the interview time, I shared my testimony of Satan's attack and the spiritual battle I had faced to shun the forces of darkness to accomplish my mission to serve and praise God in Fiji. I shared how the Lord came to my rescue and miraculously healed me by defeating Satan, who wanted to embalm me. I was excited that the whole episode turned out to be for His glory. Hundreds heard the live interview as I poured out my heart full of His grace and excellence. Later that day, I left Nadi, Fiji, to board the plane to Sydney, Australia.

Throughout my flight, I kept praising the Lord and asking Him to strengthen me so that I could perform at the last five concerts scheduled in Sydney. Satan was not yet done with me, however, and tried other tricks to obstruct my ministry. All through my trip, he kept telling me, "I will put you in a wheelchair." When I arrived in Sydney, I waited near the belt for my luggage to arrive, but it was not on the belt. So I waited for long time and could no longer stand. Satan again said, "Go and sit in the wheelchair and be comfortable." Having waited a long time for my luggage, I finally noticed the terminal was empty, and all the passengers were gone. I asked the porter about my luggage, and he said my luggage was not on this flight. I knew that was the trick Satan had played since I had put the Sydney destination tags myself on the luggage. I was exhausted and hungry and had to walk a long distance to reach the second terminal to file a complaint about my lost baggage. Satan again said to me, "You are weak and hungry; you can't walk so far. Why don't you sit in the wheelchair?" I was praying and having a spiritual battle with Satan, rebuking him, and finally, I said to him, "In the name of Jesus, I declare that you be put in the wheelchair and be put to shame forever."

The contact people were waiting for me outside to receive me, and I somehow managed to walk out to inform them about my lost luggage. It took us a couple more hours to call Suva and Fiji and get information about my luggage. I had my concert the next day, and Satan was adamant that I cancel my concert. I was exhausted, tired, and weak after the long wait at the airport. Moreover, I had no clothes, makeup, or master music tracks to perform, as all that stuff was in my suitcases. The organizers were panicking and suggested that I cancel the concert, but I knew my Lord too well and trusted Him. I left the airport without my luggage, trusting that the Lord would deliver it before my concert. The next evening, my luggage arrived on time for me to prepare for the concert. It was such a joy to perform and to share my testimony of the personal healing I had received from the Lord with all the churches. All four concerts at St. Andrews Church, Glad Tiding Church, Concord Community Church, and Fairfield Church were packed, and by His mercy, the response was tremendous. Satan's plan was thwarted, and I succeeded in sowing the seeds in Sydney and glorifying my Lord there.

Through my experiences, I learned to trust God in every situation of my life, whether in health or sickness or joy or sorrow. The truth is that the Lord is more concerned about us than we are, for He wants to be the Lord of our lives. He blessed me with a ministry and opened doors around the world to serve Him. He provided me with a new apartment and finally prompted me to pray for the new plan He had for my life.

The Lord's wooing whispers through His Word and the people he sent were instrumental in leading me through another turning point in my life. The dream revelation I had in the year 2000 when the Lord had lifted me to America was finally fulfilled into reality in the year 2004. When the Lord did another miracle in my life, it was in June when the pastor of my church in Mumbai, India, walked up to me and said, "There is a word for you," and said, "The Lord says He is building your house on a solid rock, and His glory shall shine on your face." I was perplexed as I already had a new apartment and asked the pastor what new house He was building. The pastor said, "Maybe your husband is building your house." I was confused to hear that and prayed to the Lord to seek an answer. The Lord reminded me of the dream I had four years ago of traveling in the car with my sisters and then getting stuck amidst traffic. When I got out of the car, I was lifted and taken away. I immediately knew the Lord was taking me away, just like the other dream I had of the Twin Towers and the crane lifting me to America. The only way I thought I could stay in America permanently was if the Lord had now planned for me to marry.

Knowing the nature of my God and that in Him all promises are Yes and Amen. I prayed fervently to Him. I wanted to know His will and made conditions with Him. If it was His will, He should bring a strong believer out of the blue. My second condition was if the man He brings proposes to me, it should be before the year 2004 ends. So, having said that I waited upon Him, and it was in November that David arrived in Mumbai for a short trip of nine days. I went to receive him at the airport and then dropped him off at the hotel that he had booked. For the next five days, my friend Seema and I drove him out sightseeing, shopping, and going to different restaurants and hotels so that he could enjoy and taste the variety of foods and cuisines available in Mumbai. On the sixth day, I was scheduled to be at a recording studio to work on my new album, "Tere Jaisa Koi Nahi," which means "None Like You." David was interested in my music, and he asked me if he could accompany me to hear my music and my recorded songs. I took him to the studio, where we spent the whole day. Then, by evening, we left for Seema's residence, where we were invited for supper.

On the seventh day, I was very busy and had to mix my album at the recording studio, and I didn't want David to tag around with me. I was in a fix when the spirit nudged me to take David to the Bay City Club, where I had a membership. My plan was to sign and introduce David to the manager there so that he could allow David to spend the next day at the club. As I entered the Bay City Club, the manager greeted us and showed us the new extension area that I had suggested the club's owner to add so that he can generate extra funds. It was a lavish new banquet hall that the club had recently added and decorated to rent out for weddings and parties. As we sat there, the manager spoke with us for a long time and said, "The banquet hall is all ready, but no one has yet booked the facility." I replied, "It's just beautiful; you need to do some publicity for that." Then he said, "We cannot afford that; we have already spent beyond our budget. Ma'am, I request you do that honor to inaugurate our hall. I suggest you should throw a lavish party." I hesitated, as there was no reason or occasion for me to throw the party. But he kept pursuing me by saying, "Please, Please, Ma'am, do it for me. I will handle everything for you." So finally, I agreed just to oblige him and said, "Okay, then I will throw it on the 28th." He then left to get the menu for me to help me choose the food I wanted to be catered for the banquet hall inauguration party.

When he left, David had a few moments to talk to me in private. He immediately said, "Can I ask you a question?" and I replied, "Sure." He then proposed to me by saying, "Will you marry me?" We serve the same God, Jesus. Before the manager came back, I said, "Yes" to David. He then suggested that I accompany him the next morning to select my engagement ring. The manager returned with the menu, and we decided upon the food to be catered. I was amazed to find out that the party to inaugurate the banquet hall that I planned on the 28th turned out to be my own engagement party without me being aware of it. I was taken aback as to how this could have happened without the Lord being involved in it since I had no clue that David would propose to me. All I can say is that it was His revelation that He turned into reality.

The next day, there were riots in Mumbai, and all the shops were closed, but still, my Lord made way for us to enter the jewelers' shops, and He placed everything on the platter for us. The engagement outfits and the designer rings were ready and delivered to us within a day, and the invitations were sent to the guests.

The whole engagement celebration could not have been arranged if the Lord had not intervened. Banquet halls for weddings must be booked months prior to the desired date and are never available on short notice. David had to fly out that very night of November 28th, the same date that I had scheduled the party. It would have been practically impossible by our own merit to get engaged then, but through Him and by Him, all things were possible. The whole engagement celebration was perfectly orchestrated and divinely ordained by Him.

After the celebration of the engagement party, David bid goodbye to everyone and left for the airport to board the plane to America. A month later, I arrived in America, and we were married on December 29, 2004, fulfilling the conditions I had made with the Lord. All that the Lord had shown me in my dream He finally fulfilled in my real life by relocating me to America before the end of 2004.

David was building a new house, exactly as the pastor had told me in Mumbai.

All I know is that we think the Lord may move slowly, but He moves for sure and in His own time.

There have been many other occasions when I have felt the prodding of the Lord's Spirit. The fullness of His power and richness of His mercies kept on changing the challenging situations in my life into positive accomplishments.

Life was exciting and different after marriage. I observed David working on different projects to complete the house. Designing the decor was my department, and I had a very different concept than the typical American-style decor. After much window-shopping in America, I finally decided to get Indian antique hand-carved furniture in white and gold from India, which seemed a bit irrational and expensive to David. I flew back to Mumbai to stay there for a couple of months. I had time for my furniture to be ready before I left. I ordered four end tables, a center table, a TV stand, a console, and a dressing bench. I dismantled all eight items and got them packed in my suitcases, trusting that the Lord would help me carry them on my flight back to America. So, on the day of my departure, I stood in line to check in my luggage at the Mumbai airport when the spirit nudged me to call the supervisor of the airline, whom I had not known but whose number I had gotten from a friend of mine. I then called him and informed him that I was at the airport, and he said he would meet me near the Air India counter after five minutes. The line I was waiting in was long, and fifteen minutes had already passed, but still, there was no trace of him. I waited and kept trusting the Lord.

Finally, there were only two passengers ahead of me when the luggage scale broke down. I was thrilled, thinking that I might not have to weigh my luggage, which I knew was overweight due to the heavy furniture that I had packed. After twenty minutes of delay, the machine was repaired, and it was my turn to check-in. When the porter lifted my bags onto the scale, the officer said, "You are overweight and will have to pay the fee for extra luggage." At that very moment, the supervisor I had spoken to walked in and said, "Let her go; she is my cousin." I was flabbergasted as to how the Lord had intervened to break down the machine to cause the delay so that the supervisor could arrive at the nick of the moment to let me pass through scot-free. Then, after my luggage was checked in, the supervisor offered me coffee, chatted with me for a long time, and finally walked me through, bypassing all the restrictions to board the plane. When I reached home, David was amazed that I had succeeded in getting all that furniture into my suitcases without any extra cost. It was exactly as I told him before I left for India that the Lord would send His angel to help me, as written in Exodus

23:20 "Behold, I send an Angel before you to keep you in the way and to bring you into the place which I have prepared."

There were a lot of other things pending that I needed to accomplish in America since my initial priority after marriage had just been to fulfill my concert assignments. Three and a half years had passed, and I had still not applied for my green card, as I had been going in and out of the U.S. for my concert trips. It was in July 2008 that I finally applied for a marriage-based green card and was soon scheduled for an interview at the local United States Citizenship and Immigration Services office. David had gathered all the valid documents and certificates needed to verify that we were legally married and had been living together for the last three and a half years at the same residence. As I was about to depart, the spirit clearly nudged me to carry all my music materials, such as albums, files, and concert fliers, with me. I told David that I needed to take my music material along with me, which seemed silly to him. He thought all that material would not help prove the validity of our marriage, and it made no sense to him. I agreed with him and thought he was right, but I was still adamant and didn't want to rebel against the instruction of the spirit, so I took everything and placed it in our car.

When we reached the USCIS office, we waited for our turn to be called in. Finally, our names were called.

The officers there seemed very traditional and conservative in their thinking. The lady officer who interviewed me appeared very strict, and her aggressive style of cross-questioning confused and intimidated me. She examined all the documents David had brought to prove the validity of our marriage, but she was still not satisfied. Her main concern was why I had delayed procuring a green card for three and a half years, which I should have obtained immediately after my marriage. Her other concern was why I, being an immigrant spouse, had left the country umpteen times without prior permission from the authorities. I tried to convince her, but nothing worked until I placed all my albums, concert fliers, and files in front of her. She was pretty amazed and fascinated seeing my concert fliers and proof of me serving the Lord and spreading the gospel around the world. Her attitude then changed, and without saying or questioning me further, she quietly opened my passport and stamped it, approving my application. Within a few months, I received my green card. By paying attention and obeying the inner voice without rebelling, I foolishly took the fliers and succeeded in accomplishing my mission.

Prayer can bring magnificent transformations and breakthroughs in your life, but we need to pray in faith for revelations to come into reality. Hebrews 11:1 "Now faith is the substance of things hoped for, the evidence of things not seen." By faith, you can achieve, receive, and rise high, for you have no limit. Prayer also has the power to destroy the enemy's plan to attack you. There have been so many times when the Holy Spirit has nudged me to pray. Knowing that there is a specific reason to pray, I have been obedient and have succeeded in destroying the plan of the enemy, which could have been fatal.

It was Sunday morning when David and I got dressed to leave for church. I decided that I would drive that morning. While driving, I was chatting with David and suggested that we buy a new car, maybe my favorite Mercedes. He replied, "Why would I buy that expensive car? I will think about it later." I said, "But I know God will supply it soon, according to His glorious riches in Jesus Christ." As I drove further, I asked David, "Is this the next turn towards the church?" But he did not respond, so when I drove ahead by missing the turn, he violently turned my wheel towards the left in a jiffy, and my car headed on top of the curb, and again, he rashly returned the wheel towards the left, and the car headed straight into the path of the speeding cars from the opposite direction. I was shocked, shaky, and nervous as chills ran through my body, holding on to the wheel that he twisted unawares. Soon, a thick black cloud covered the front screen of my car, making me blind and panicky. It was as if some truck had dashed against me, and I could not discern what was happening and where I was. I believe it was the airbag that had blasted. The car then skidded and landed with a huge jerk, making a scary screeching sound into the open yard of someone's bungalow. I was shocked, dazed, and blank, unable to look beyond, when suddenly, an elderly lady knocked on my car window. I then got back to my senses and observed the blood oozing out of my palm like a shower. David observed it and tried to press my hand hard to stop it with his hurtful thumb. The neighbors then all rushed out to help us, as well as the people from the opposite cars. Soon, the ambulance arrived, and we were admitted to the hospital, which was next to our crash site. Satan's plan for that morning was thwarted, and so also was David's.

Ever since I was married to David, he had never thought about two primary things that any other husband would want for his newly married wife to attain. Primarily, the Citizenship of America, which he never wanted me to have, contesting with me that it does not have any benefits besides the authority to vote. My Green Card was sufficient for him. Secondarily, he did not want me to obtain a driver's license. The major things that every man would want for his wife's security and self-sufficiency in a new country like America. But his good intentions for me proved it all.

Anyway, by God's grace, the car crash actually turned out to be a boon in disguise for me. The insurance company paid us more than we expected, and the Lord got me the best car of my choice.

Having accepted the Lord, Christianity taught me how to walk in faith and follow God's commandments. The Bible clearly speaks about the greatest commandment of God is "Love," and that is so true. I diligently paid the vows by loving my husband and being faithful to him. The verse in Ecclesiastes 9:9 says, "Enjoy life with your wife, whom you love, all the days of this meaningless life that God has given you under the sun-all your meaningless days. For this is your lot in life and toilsome labor."

I do believe God is love, and love is God. Anyone who does not love is not of God. There is no other treasure beyond and above love that makes you happy to satisfy the thirst of the longing soul. As for my life, I thought at one moment I had it all: name, fame, money, and love. But that was just vanity and a temporary illusion of mine. The only guy who ever loved me desperately and intensely was Chintu, who died for me because he could not marry me. But the man who got me as a wife and married me failed miserably to be able to love me as his wife. All I can say is that I am still rich in love as a tycoon in Christ. For His unending showered love on me has been more than enough to fuel my life with joy and happiness till eternity.

CHAPTER 8

EMBRACING THE VOID

My personal life had been in the doldrums for a very long time. Being a prayer warrior, I decided to fight my personal battles to rid myself of the stuff that had killed me inside. I was sick of all the past baggage and the toxic tapes that kept on rewinding in my mind. I wanted to delete all and start afresh, knowing that the purpose of my life was not to cry and crib over spilled milk, nor to pacify myself in self-pity, but to work according to His will to achieve greater heights. So, in the solitary, secluded silence of my soul, I declared freedom from the walls and wounds. I closed my prayer room door, fell at His feet, and cried out to Him, asking, "Why me Lord? Why did You make me a sacrificial lamb to suffer for my husband's sin?" He was silent and spoke not a word. I then opened my Bible to hear Him speak, and the verse whispered, "Yet as a man suffers as a Christian, let him not be ashamed, but let him glorify God on his behalf." My heart pounded, and I realized the anguish and hurt that I had endured had a purpose to glorify God. The scars that pained my heart now carried a pen in my thoughts to accomplish my goal.

My pen moved and my painful testimonies sprouted and bloomed to transform itself into the story of my book that oriented me to the position where the Lord desired me to be. For the Lord always leads you where you need to be.

Thus, being commissioned for a purpose, I got totally engrossed in my book, which not only worked as a perfect therapy but also helped me to escape from the deep, dark void that I was in. So, being highly motivated, I devoted maximum time to writing so that I could complete my book soon. When all of a sudden, the Lord withdrew His anointing and inspiration from me to write further. I felt helpless, exactly as Samson felt, whose strength was gone when Delilah had cut off his locks. However, later, he waited and regained his strength till his hair grew back. Likewise, I also struggled hard to regain my passion and strength to work on my book but failed to write further. Fearing the fact that I would be back in the same rut, I asked the Lord to rejuvenate me afresh, and the Spirit within me confirmed "Hold on - you have many more testimonies to add." Though I was flabbergasted, I was fully content to know that God was faithful and had an initiative and a direction for my book. Thus, having known what the destiny of my book was, I decided to set it aside and went on to face the dark reality of my life that

I had always tried to escape from. When we are hurting, it is not uncommon to look for ways to fill the void. It was tough for me to embrace the void and live an empty life of loneliness that I had been living. The joy of my life had been diminishing like the flame of a lamp, and the wick had no more fuel in the reservoir to keep the flame burning. I then tried to distract myself from my feelings before I could get burnt out. There was something in me that had been broken, damaged, and unrepairable. I was insecure and felt I was not whole, yet I could not do anything to complete myself. I tried to manipulate myself to cover the pain I had suffered. I jumped into distractions, trying to pack my schedule with work, things, friends, shopping sprees, and doing chores at home and for others. Yet all was in vain. The hard work stressed me out, and avoiding, neglecting, and hiding my worries only doubled my trouble.

I could not accept or come to terms with the fact that I had to be with myself only, without any other person or thing to fill the void of my heart and soul. The dream that I had since I was a young maiden to live a bubbly life full of joy, happiness, companionship, and fulfillment with my better half was lost and crushed. Satan had stolen that other part of me and sucked the very joy out of my life. On the other hand, I believe nothing ever crossed David's mind, nor did any part of him feel that way or perceived how I was dying an emotional death. All I saw was him being happy, content, and complete in himself, enjoying and leading a merry, blissful life of ignorance.

I always slept upstairs in the bedroom, while David preferred sleeping downstairs in the living room on the recliner. I believe the TV and laptop were his preferences above me. Although that was sad and hurtful and not right in the sight of the Lord, I lived with that lifestyle for years. I never confronted him, fought, or ever questioned him as to why he was sleeping downstairs and was awake till late hours at night. My only weapon was to trust and pray to the Lord, for it was not my battle but His.

It was a cold winter night, and it was snowing hard. I was sleeping in my bedroom upstairs when suddenly it seemed like I was shaken, so I got up with a jerk and tried to sleep again, but I failed since the lights in the living room downstairs were on. Then, I walked down the staircase and observed David being busy with the laptop. I went back to my bed and tried to catch my sleep when the Holy Spirit nudged me to go and confront him. I was too scared to walk down the staircase. Then Satan warned me of the repercussions I would face. I retreated and walked back up to my bed. Having walked downstairs and upstairs a couple of times, I watched the time, and it was past 3:00 a.m. I wrestled within myself and with the Spirit, as I was indecisive because of the fear that had gripped me. The Spirit was still stern and persistent, and the power was so strong on me that I finally regained my guts. I walked straight up to David and asked him what he was doing so late in the night. He coolly shut off his laptop and said, "Nothing, just playing games." Then I walked up to my bedroom, and again, the Spirit gave me the exact words I needed to go and tell him. I then came down again and said, "You prayed to God asking Him to give you a wife, and He gave you what you desired, but now you have rejected God by rejecting what He gave you and have chosen what Satan has to offer you." He was quiet and listened to all that I had to say. Later, I suggested to him that we discuss our problems with the pastor and seek his help, but he shrugged me off and said, "I am not going to do that." I tried my best to convince him, but he was adamant and presumptuous about what I said, and denied my request. He said, "Nothing will ever change between us, even if I give up on everything."

So, I left and walked up to my bedroom. The whole episode was too disrespectful, and I was distressed physically and emotionally. I knew Satan had attacked our marriage and hindered our relationship. For James 4:7 says, "Submit yourselves therefore to God. Resist the devil, and he will flee from you." I was worried and restless, tossing and turning on my bed, apprehensive of the consequences when suddenly it seemed like someone had pounced on me. The weight was too heavy to bear. I felt choked and unable to breathe. Chills passed through my body, scaring me, and I started trembling. Having struggled for a long and being unable to get rid of the crushing weight on me, I started rebuking it in the name of Jesus to depart from me. A distressing emotion arose within me that nauseated me. Then I ran downstairs to the bathroom to throw up. David was nervous to see my debilitating condition and walked me up to my bedroom. He put lots of blankets on me so that my shivering could stop. Then we both prayed till the Evil One departed, and I fell asleep.

The next day, I did exactly what the Spirit wanted me to do. I went to meet the church elder and shared with him that we were having problems in our marriage. After meeting with David, the elder advised David that we both needed to go for marriage counseling, so we did what was needed. During our counseling sessions, David explained the problem we were having in our marriage. He confessed that he did not have the kind of emotions that he should have for this marriage. I had a sinking feeling in my stomach as I heard him say that, and tears started dripping from my eyes. I felt sorry that he had failed God and disobeyed His commandment, as it says in Ephesians 5:25, "Husbands, love, your wives, even as Christ also loved the church, and gave himself for it." I then told the counselor that I had a gut feeling that he had been having a love affair with someone else, but David denied that accusation. Then, after we left the counselor's office, David said, "I hope these sessions work, but if they don't, I have a different strategy." As we drove back in the car, he said,

"I am not in love with anyone else. I just know one thing, that you are my wife and my only wife, period."

The mere title "wife" was not good enough for me to make me feel happy as his wife. I believed happiness consisted of at least three good things: something to do, something to love, and something to look forward to. Living just a life all by myself, there was nothing for me to do, love, or look forward to. My dream and desire was to do all those things with my best friend and partner. But on the other hand, since David was an introvert, he was happy being all by himself and fully content with himself. He seemed detached and often oblivious to his surroundings. Being secluded and withdrawn made him feel secure in his own comfort zone. He preferred staying in the reserved propitious ambiance of his own world. We were just two sides of the same coin, being joined and yet apart. He opted to be busy with his job, friends, church, activities, golf, health issues, commitments, and Gideon's ministry. Having too many things spinning in his mind, it was very easy for him to take me for granted and drop me off the list.

Days, months, and years passed by, but our relationship stood still. Neither of us complained, discussed, or even desired to bring up the topic. Dealing with it would only cause more conflict, time, and energy. The only best way out was to go through the charade of pretending that our marriage was just perfect.

2 Corinthians 5:15 says, "And he died for all, that they which live should not henceforth live unto themselves, but unto him, which died for us and rose again." The Bible verse spoke to me and comforted me, and I realized God did not redeem me in order to fill my life with the stuff that I desired, like our pleasures, passions, desires, and dreams. For He, being a mighty God, had much greater plans for me. He wanted me to be a vessel of honor to live my life for His glory, but as I am writing this book, I realize that if my personal life had been stable and without any trials and tribulations, this book would have had no story. Life is not an easy way, but rather, it has a way of beating and robbing us of our joy. Amidst all those trials, Jesus finally reveals His purpose. Most of the best people in the Bible had terrible lives. Paul was in peril and prison. Shadrach, Meshach, and Abednego were thrown into a fiery furnace. Jonah was imperiled by the storm. Joseph was sold by his brothers into slavery, and Job lost all his cattle, children, health and wealth. Yet they all waited on the Lord in faith and made history by being the most noble characters in the Bible.

Being in a similar situation of pain and trials, the Lord commanded me to pack my bags and leave for India immediately. I was obedient to Him and booked a return ticket from Chicago to Mumbai and back to Chicago. All through my flight, I could not discern why the Lord wanted me to leave in such a jiffy. When I reached Mumbai, everything changed, and I had all the time to myself and for my ministry. There were no household chores for me to do or any meals to cook; my servants did it all, and I got everything on a platter. I felt free and uplifted as I didn't have to bear the brunt of loneliness that had left deep scars within me. Nobody tried to ignore me. My family and friends loved me. I was respected in all the churches where I ministered and in the slum areas where I shared the love of God with the poor and needy. People loved me and my music and desired that I visit them again, so all that helped me to recoup mentally and emotionally. During that time, David was constantly in touch with me and always expressed that he was doing fine and managing well on his own. Unfortunately, I never heard him say, "I miss you."

I was happy he was doing fine till one day when he shocked me with bad news. He called me up to inform me that he had a serious accident and had undergone major surgery. He explained that he tripped and had fallen in the basement of our house, then he fell twice at his friend's place and later fell for the fourth time at home, squatting on the floor. That had torn the tendons apart in both of his knees, for which he had to be operated upon immediately. He further stated that the surgery went off well, and his brother had volunteered to stay and take care of him. When I heard his story, I was terrified and shocked. I told him, "I am going to take the first flight to be with you." He then insisted that I should not change my flight date, explaining that I would be of no help to him, and suggested that it would be best if I returned on my scheduled date. After we hung up, I was in tears and felt guilty for not being with him. I kept praying diligently and in faith, trusting that the Lord would restore him back to normalcy. That was the moment I realized why the Lord commanded me to leave for India. For He very well knew I was weak, broken, and lacked the physical and emotional resilience to face any more trauma. I arrived back home at the perfect time when his brother was gone. Meanwhile, David had started doing his basic chores and had also started his therapy sessions so that he could recoup fast. Thus, the gracious God worked on him and blessed him to resume his work back during winter.

CHAPTER 9

THE UNTIED MARRIAGE KNOT

"So I gave them up into their own heart's lust, and they walked in their own counsels."

– Psalm 81:12

Winter has its own charm. It's one of the most awesome seasons, and it sparkles God's glory lavishly through its white, crystal-clear snow, depicting His sanctity and unblemished purity around us. Every rooftop, tree, and yard seems like it is covered by the showers of His blessings, which makes you feel like you are placed in a Holy wonderland. The same awesome winter can also be harsh on you, too, when the Lord thunders the storm and gusty winds lash across your face. It was one of those thunderous days when a warning had been issued about a severe blizzard coming our way. I was worried as David had not yet fully recouped and had to walk through the white-out conditions and the slippery, icy roads to reach his workplace. Moreover, we had no extra cell phones, so I suggested that he buy an iPhone to carry along as a safety measure. He did what was needed, and I was very pleased that he could now reach me in case an emergency arose. Little did I know that the same gadget that I got David to protect him from the snow was none other than a weapon for Satan to do a snow job. While I had the responsibility to manage the household affairs and to work on my book, David had no job responsibility as he was on leave recouping. Thus, all through the harsh winter, we were both homebound. The only recreation David had was to either watch TV or invent new games to play on his cell. Thus, Satan cunningly entered into our married life to drift us apart by luring and enticing David to go his way. Although I was unaware of it, all that came to my knowledge on a Sunday morning in the church prayer room. When I left for the restroom and returned after a few seconds, I noticed David messaging on his cell and instantly trying to skulk it away behind his back as he observed me walking back into the prayer room. Then I got suspicious and questioned him, why are you hiding your phone in your hands? Then, after a long discussion, he confessed that he was communicating with his old friends, whom he had known prior to our marriage.

Meanwhile, the church service started, so I left the prayer room to attend. Later, David walked in for the service after deleting all the messages and softly said, "You can have the phone." I replied to him and said, "No, thanks, I don't need it now." I was traumatized that he had been cheating on me. Soon, his tactics became more conspicuous to me as I had never seen his phone placed in my house nor had I heard it ring. On most of our trips, he never entertained any calls. He usually left me alone in the hotel rooms pretending to go for a early breakfast, for a morning walk, or sometimes to read his Bible in the hotel lobby so that he could chat freely with his friends. Once, when His phone vibrated, I said to him, "Why don't you respond to your message? I know it's from your friend." He got upset and said, "You can think what you want. I don't give a damn." It was too humiliating for me to know that he could go to such extremes. My hopes, dreams, and wishes I had left back in India, but not my self-esteem and dignity. Expecting faithfulness and exclusivity of priority above others was my legal right as a wife and not just an obligation. Giving priority to his friends in his life, over and above me, was too much to handle. I decided to walk out gracefully and started planning to leave for India, but I had to wait until my yearly medical checkups were completed.

Finally, I was done with my checkups that were scheduled at the Clinic. So, after my checkup, I left to meet him in his office, where he asked me to meet him. When I entered his office, he immediately stood up to greet me and suggested that we go to the cafeteria for a cup of coffee. I waited for a moment before we could leave and observed my photo missing from his desk. We then left for the cafeteria and returned back home. Days passed by, but I never questioned him about my missing photo. I was hurt and knew he had probably torn it and thrown it away. But to my satisfaction, I asked him, "How come my photo was missing from your desk?" He bluntly replied, "I don't know anything about it. Somebody must have taken it away, or maybe you stole it." I was appalled by his accusation, for it is written in Proverbs "Lying lips are an abomination to the Lord, but those who act faithfully are His delight." Nevertheless, by not being faithful to me, he succeeded in ruining our relationship. The message was clear that he detested seeing my photo on his table and wanted it to be out of his sight. Then, how much more detestable I was to him in person.

I could no longer overlook the manner in which he tried to emotionally abuse and hurt me. I had reached a saturation point. The hurt depressed me, and depression added disappointment and disappointment added stress to my life. That made it impossible for me to leave for my ministry concerts, as I was unable to prioritize them over and above my dwindling marriage. Satan had made me miserable and had succeeded in stopping my ministry. He had entered into our married life by causing David to drift away from me to his evil way, by taking him into his dark, secluded corner and enticing him to lead a life of secrecy, deception, and denial. I kept praying for him, knowing that he was not walking in the way of the Lord. Satan had simply blinded him, and he could not see or understand his folly. I could not chasten him and left him in the Lord's hands to open his eyes.

It was a Saturday afternoon incident that occurred between David and me that compelled me in my spirit to withdraw completely from him. I finally decided to give him all the time and space he required to do whatever his heart desired. Psalm 81:12 says it all, "So I gave them up into their own hearts lust and they walked in their own counsels."

The people of Israel did not submit to the Lord, so He gave them over to their stubborn hearts to follow their own devices. Thus, I did the same to let go of him in his stubborn way and announced, "As far as I am concerned, I have set you free. You are a free bird from now onwards. You don't need to hide your phone from me anymore. You can do whatever you want, with whom you want, and whenever you want freely and openly in front of me. I then walked out of his bedroom. From that day on, I emotionally and mentally untied my marriage knot from him. I never cared about his phone, what he did, or to whom he spoke. I had my self-esteem and didn't want to stoop low to know, see, or deal with what he did. 1 Corinthians 6:9-10 says, "Know ye not that the unrighteous shall not inherit the kingdom of God? Be not deceived: neither fornicators, nor idolaters, nor adulterers, nor effeminate, nor abusers of themselves with mankind, nor thieves nor covetous, nor drunkards, nor revilers, nor extortioners shall inherit the kingdom of God."

Although I had withdrawn myself completely from David, my war was not yet over. As a matter of fact, I started my spiritual warfare through prayer to bring his every thought into captivity to the obedience of Christ. The Bible says in 2 Corinthians 10:3-5, "For though we walk in the flesh: we do not war after the flesh: For the weapons of our warfare are not carnal, but mighty through God to the pulling down of strong holds; casting down imaginations, and every high thing that exalted itself against the knowledge of God, and bringing into captivity every thought to the obedience of Christ."

In the meantime, I kept searching for the best flight deals and finally booked my ticket to leave for Mumbai. Soon, the departure date arrived, and David drove me off to Chicago O'Hare International Airport. I left after I had passed through the immigration clearance. When I boarded the plane, I reminisced about the whole scene of David standing afar from me to bid me adieu at the airport while other passengers sobbed, kissed, and hugged as their loved ones departed. All that saddened me to watch how a loving husband of mine had been deprived and incapacitated to give me even a formal hug. The message was clear that he had lost it all, his integrity, his loyalty, his fidelity, and his benevolence towards his wife. My heart simply cried for him as he chose to walk in his way and not in the ways of the Lord.

Having arrived in Mumbai, I could finally take a sigh of relief being out of this rut. During the day, I worked on my music, did the ministry work, and completed unfinished album projects that had to be dubbed and mixed. Evening times I spent with my sisters and friends by going out to different restaurants for meals, watching movies, going for long drives, or sometimes hanging out till late at night with friends at the beachfront cafeterias. Life was much different for me in Mumbai than in Wisconsin since most of the people there are habituated to enjoy doing stuff till late evenings. The streets are fully lit up with the passing cars and autos hustling, bustling, and honking out loud. The pubs, bars, and restaurants are noisy and jam-packed with customers. The people are seen walking past midnight hours on the beachfront, and some hover in and out of ice cream parlors for their favorite drinks and treats. All that hectic life was quite a change for me to be out of my secluded Wisconsin life.

David, being an introvert, loved a secluded life, yet he was constantly in touch with me on WhatsApp. After a couple of months, I started receiving e-mails from him, expressing his desire to work on our relationship. One of his e-mails was as follows:

"Dear Kadambari,

I am impressed what I am reading in the Love and Respect book. Last summer, when we started counseling, I decided that you are my wife, period...forever, and I have no reason to think any other way. I do not see the reason we cannot learn from these books and talk to each other about the things we need to break out of these cycles we are in. I am very optimistic that we can and will overcome our issues and go forward with a much more enjoyable relationship with each other. I love you, and you love me. I want good for you, and you want good for me. You are very important to me, very important. We have the basis to build on, and I look forward to your return so we can continue to improve together. Love you, take care of you. Kiss. David"

After getting a lot of lovey-dovey e-mails from him, I was in a fix, wondering what issues he was talking about. We had no issue except that we had no relationship between us whatsoever.

Yet, being his wife, I opted to stay with him and was not self-seeking but faithful as the Lord would want me to be. The Bible verse says the virtues of love are priceless and love keeps no records of wrongs, as explained in 1 Corinthians 13:4-7, "Love is patient, love is kind. It does not envy, it does not boast, and it is not proud. It does not dishonor others, it is not easily angered, and it keeps no record of wrongs. Love does not delight in evil but rejoices with the truth. It always protects, always trusts, always hopes, and always perseveres."

So, after receiving many more positive e-mails from David, I kept my ego on the shelf and returned back home. Surprisingly, after my return, David did not change a wee bit. The same detached pattern continued in our marriage as we went on to live our lives. He failed to honor all that he wrote in the e-mails by being dismissive. So I decided not to waver and hobble anymore between two opinions, wondering whether he cared for me or not. I understood his plan to have it both ways: living indecisively in a neutral zone on the one hand and pretending to be committed to me on the other. It takes two hands to clap together and, likewise, two wheels of the cart to be in sync to keep the cart moving. I could not sustain keeping the cart moving any longer, as it seemed that was not his heart's desire.

The Lord definitely knew his heart's desire and all that was in store for me, so He had specifically instructed me in Mumbai to obtain my U.S. citizenship as soon as I got back to the U.S. I told David exactly what the Lord had asked me to do, but he was reluctant and kept arguing, stating that citizenship would not benefit me in any manner, except to give me the right to vote. Trusting the Lord more than him, I finally told him, "You don't have to decide for me; I will decide for myself." So, I went ahead with the naturalization process to obtain my citizenship.

A couple of months had passed, and there was nothing on David's list to discuss regarding his plan. Finally, it was on a Saturday evening when I initiated the conversation with him. I told him, "It's been a long time since I arrived, and I have noticed you have been occupied with your activities. I think you wanted to work on our relationship as you had written to me saying that we need to get out of those cycles that we both were in." He immediately changed his color, got upset, and said, "Are you trying to put me down?" I was startled by his response and was dismayed by his attack. For in no manner did I think that I was trying to put him down? Rather, my heart was to resolve our issues in a swift and amicable manner, as he had expressed earlier to me in his e-mail. So, I raised the white flag but later regretted the same.

I was unable to discern what was on his mind and within his heart. I was confused by his dual/split personality. My life began to crumble around me. On one of those rough nights, I had a dream, and in my dream, I saw numerous poisonous snakes, venomous black spiders, and large scorpions struggling to creep out of a multitude of small holes in our bedroom walls, but I saw the most ferocious lion locked in a cage at the end of our bedroom. 1st Peter 5:8 says, "Be sober, be vigilant; because your adversary the devil, a roaring lion, walketh about, seeking whom he may devour." The vicious, creepy dream I had elicited a deadly fear within me and repulsed me to see the eerie creatures emitting their negative vibes in our bedroom. But the adversary, the devil, being locked in the cage, was deprived of devouring me, assuring me that I was safe. The next day, I shared that dream with David, but he was unable to know what the spirit was trying to convey or warn me about.

After a couple of days, on Friday, August 7th, after supper, David suggested that he wanted to talk to me and finally opened his Pandora box. He expressed that he had lived a miserable and frustrating life with me for the past so many years. He further stated that he had decided to take some drastic steps and mentioned that he had met a lawyer to discuss the no-fault divorce. All this came as a surprise to me out of the blue, that he had finally made this inevitable decision on his own. The inveterate contempt that he had towards me, which had frustrated him for years, finally spilled out of his mouth, exactly like my dream of the poisonous eerie creatures struggling to come out of the holes. The revelation that I had became a reality. Soon, I started looking for a good lawyer and worked on winding up my life in the U.S.

It was very tough for me to move back to Mumbai after ten years. I had too much stuff to carry back home. David suggested that it would be much easier for me if I just walked away, leaving all my personal belongings behind, which he could then discard for me or distribute to his family members. He specifically also made it clear to me, saying, "I will no more be responsible for you from now onwards. You have to be on your own." I knew he wanted me to be out of our house. I was ready to be out, but I preferred not to leave behind a single trace of mine for him to see or remember that I ever existed in his life. So, I put all my personal belongings on sale at my residence and at fairs. I gave away all my winter clothing to friends free of cost and donated bags and bags full of stuff to Saint Vincent DePaul. All of my other expensive items and designer outfits that I had collected throughout the years from different parts of the world were sold at the price of pennies.

I threw away my concert fliers, my appreciation letters, my interview chat-backs, and concert video recordings, sold my musical instruments, and tore up all my contacts' address diaries. All the memorable photographs that I had treasured for years, including the moments that I had spent with David, I tore into bits and dumped them into the trash. Plus, I gave away hundreds of my recorded compact discs, as it was impossible to carry too much baggage with me. I shut down my Garden of Renown International Ministry, which had been registered with the state of Wisconsin, and closed my bank account. I resigned from my Church's mission committee and discontinued being a Gideon International auxiliary member. I was mentally and emotionally drained, distraught, and broken.

I had to arrange for a place to move in and for the funds to pay my lawyer upfront. My friends were kind and volunteered to drive me to my lawyer's appointments and helped me search for rentals to accommodate me, but unfortunately, none were available. So we had to visit different shelter homes of the destitute where woman abandoned by their husbands stayed. My heart sank as I entered one of the shelter homes, thinking how David had brought me to such a low level. I waited for the lady in charge of the shelter, who later called me in. She interviewed me and asked me where I lived, who I was, and what I did. After learning that I was an international gospel singer and had served the Lord by ministering to people around the world, she finally questioned me: "Why would a lady like you want to come and stay here? After she said that, I was unable to control the intense emotions of my grieving heart and broken spirit.

I fell flat on her desk feeling indignant and wept bitterly as I kept narrating to her the story of my pain and suffering being lonely, devoid of everything, and having no one or no place to go anywhere. She then hugged me close to her as she heard my pathetic story. As I left her office, she said, "I will inform you as soon as the vacancy occurs." Later, she prayed and said, "You look like a very dignified woman of faith, and none of my inmates here have faith like yours. May your Lord God be with you."

David observed silently how miserable I was and all that I had been going through. He knew I had been struggling to sort out my things but never commented, reacted, or expressed any remorse about it. It was Friday afternoon when he came home for lunch and asked me if I was free to talk with him tonight after supper. I told him surely we can talk. So after supper, we both settled down to talk, and he said, "I have no plan to divorce you, and I have decided that I will not divorce you." I got very upset with him for all that he made me go through. Primarily, he expressed to all his family and friends that the major problem with our divorce was that we had nothing in common, and secondarily, we had cultural differences. Perhaps he was unaware that marriage is a relationship in which you evolve gradually when you overlook your differences and invest quality time in building your relationship. I was very upset since cultural differences were not the real cause of our divorce. Moreover, knowing the guts he had to invalidate his own statement made things worse. Still, we had nothing in common, and neither did our cultural differences evaporate. Then I replied back and said to him, "You may not divorce me, but I will show you, how I will divorce you now. For what you started, I will finish now."

I was desperate to get away from David as he made me go through hell. I was very keen to leave for India but had no way out. I was stuck as I could not leave the country and had to wait for the final interview call from the USCIS before I could be a U.S. citizen. So, I delayed serving the divorce papers to David. But he had already met with his lawyers and finalized the formalities. So, after a while, he made it clear to me and said, "I don't think you need to wait for your citizenship anymore since you won't be staying in the U.S. and will be leaving soon for India. I suggest that you waste no more time and that you better move ahead with the divorce."

So, on September 30th, I finally served him with the divorce papers. I knew marriage was the testimony of my life for God's glory, but divorce was not the Lord's plan for me. I asked for forgiveness from the Lord as I had failed Him miserably. But since David made me suffer to extremes, made me walk through water and fire, and later had the audacity to turn around to withdraw the divorce, it bugged me a lot. It was like adding more fuel to the fire. I thought I was not a puppet in his hand, and he had no right or power to play with my life and my emotions... period. So it was in my pride I gave him back what he had desired and deserved.

In the meantime, our lawyers worked together according to the legal formalities to sort things out between them. Later, they had individual meetings with us to make the settlement amicable. We both were simultaneously negotiating upon the said terms, as the final date to appear in the court, November 20th, to sign the divorce decree was approaching.

During that time, I received a letter from the USCIS in Minneapolis that my final appointment for an interview had been scheduled, but David disagreed to drive me, suggesting that it made no sense to report there now, as I would be leaving soon for India. So, I was unable to go to the USCIS office. The Lord instructed me to get citizenship, but Satan obstructed me from obtaining it.

Time was passing by, and the divorce date was approaching. I was nervous as divorce had a domino effect on me, turning my world upside down. Every area of my life was disrupted and in chaos; nothing meant anything to me anymore. I felt like a dry leaf being carried away by the turbulent storm, having no control to evade the calamity that was to come. Having been in the midst of a grieving process due to David's betrayal, I found myself in the deepest, darkest valley of my life, and for the first time, I began to question God, "Where are you, Lord? What did I do to deserve this?" I knew I had to face it and had no other option to evade the hour that was to come on me. So, like a sheep ready for the slaughter, I had to capitulate to face the dreaded day of betrayal on November 20th, exactly as Jesus faced. Remembering that He also was betrayed by Judas the same way and was too weak to face the situation, wanting the cup to pass away from Him as mentioned in Matthew 26:38-48, "Then saith He unto them, My soul is exceedingly sorrowful even unto death: tarry ye here, and watch with me. And he went a little further and fell on his face, and prayed, saying, O my Father, if it be possible, let this cup pass from me: nevertheless, not as I will, but as thou wilt. And he cometh unto his disciples, and findeth them asleep, and saith unto Peter, What could ye not watch with me one hour? Watch and pray that ye enter not into temptation: the spirit indeed is willing, but the flesh is weak. He went out again the second time and prayed, saying, O my Father, if this cup may not pass away from me, except I drink it, thy will be done. And he came and found them asleep again: for their eyes were heavy, and he left them and went away again, and prayed the third time, saying the same words. Then cometh he to his disciples and saith unto them, sleep on now, and take your rest: behold the hour is at hand, and the son of man is betrayed unto the hands of the sinner. Rise, let us be going: behold, he is at hand that doth betray me."

I decided that I needed to align my life with Jesus as the dreaded day was approaching fast. I prayed to the Father, replicating Jesus. Though I was mentally, physically, and emotionally bankrupt, spiritually, I was rich as a tycoon in God, trusting and claiming the Bible verse in Psalm 40:1-3,

“

"I waited patiently for the Lord;
And He inclined unto me,
And heard my cry.
He also brought me up out of a horrible pit,
Out of the miry clay,
And set my feet upon a rock,
And established my steps.
He has put a new song in my mouth-
Praise to our God;
Many will see it and fear
And will trust in the Lord."

”

Thus, by faith, I believe that any tragic event of our life can only be unbearable if we aren't sure that our God is for us and with us through thick and thin, through joy and pain, and through loss and gain. For 1 Peter 4:16 says, "Yet if any man suffers as a Christian, let him not be ashamed; but let him glorify God on this behalf."

Similarly, as I am writing this book of mine, I am not ashamed to wash my dirty linen in public. I have realized that suffering is actually the heart of my story. Being a strong woman of faith, Christianity has empowered me to sit strong in the midst of my life's crisis, to trust and taste the glory of God's faithfulness. It has also taught me to rejoice in anticipation over the forthcoming reward of His divine intervention.

CHAPTER 10

ROMAN HOLIDAY

"For I, the Lord thy God, will hold thy right hand, saying unto thee, Fear not; I will help thee."

– Isaiah 41:13

It was November the 7th, a chilly wintry afternoon when I was rejoicing and praising the Lord while seated on my recliner, curled up in my blankie when suddenly the whispering sound of the wind caught my attention. I gazed outside my window and observed through Mother Nature the mystical vision of God's beauty as soft snow flurries kept falling gently from the dark clouded sky. The frost had already covered and hidden the edges of my window, and the frozen silvery icicles flaunted their gorgeous glow from the top of my neighbor's eaves. But the large, naked, sturdy deciduous trees in my yard that had been stripped of all their leaves and beauty still stood proud and erect without any shame, juxtaposing how I had similarly been stripped of all. Most probably waiting in faith to be exuberantly adorned back into summer, just to remind me that my summer was also not very far away.

Suddenly, my phone distracted me, and it was my lawyer at the other end who said, "I have good news to share. Your divorce settlement agreement has been memorialized with David, and I was anxious to know if you wanted me to negotiate any further." I then asked him if he had negotiated with him about my alimony since David had specifically made it clear that from now on, I would have to be on my own, and he would no longer be responsible for me. Having heard me say that, he got very upset and said, "I have not yet discussed that with David, but what makes him think that you are no longer his responsibility? You are still his wife and legally entitled to stay in your own house till the divorce decree is issued. If David has a problem with you, then ask him to leave the house." Then, he discussed the additional benefits that I would receive as a U.S. citizen. I then explained to him that I would not be entitled to those benefits, for as per the USCIS rules, the money gets forfeited and the application dismissed if you fail to appear for the final citizenship interview and do not get it rescheduled within the 30-day time frame. He then said, "I suggest you somehow try to reschedule your interview first. Are you going to leave all your benefits on the table and walk away? Since I am your lawyer, it's my duty to protect you and your future. Citizenship has to be your first priority for your security and health benefits, and I want you to obtain it immediately. It won't hurt anyone to delay the divorce date further. I don't want you to appear in court on November 20th. I am going to take the next court date and will inform you later." Then, after he hung up the phone, I took a sigh of relief. I immediately realized why the Lord had insisted that I acquire my citizenship as soon as I reached the U.S.A. Although I was unable to discern the whole mystery behind the Lord's plan at that moment in Mumbai, one thing was for sure - he made me escape the day that I dreaded the most. For 1 Peter 1: 6-7 says, "In this, you greatly rejoice, though now for a little while, if need be, you have been grieved by various trials, that the genuineness of your faith, being much more precious than gold that perishes, though it is tested by fire, may be found to praise, honor, and glory at the revelation of Jesus Christ."

Then, I started rejoicing, trusting that in God's drama, unparalleled distress can set a perfect stage for unparalleled deliverance. For somewhere within me, I had the assurance that, as a strong believer, as I walked through the dark tunnel, the light surely awaited me on the other side. Since the divorce date was averted, I was at peace, but deep inside me, I still had the fear of facing the next court date, which hung like a sword over my head. Nevertheless, I was still very happy, thanking God for stalling the dreadful day. It was nearing 4 p.m., and I received a call from David reminding me to be ready to attend an event that evening. It was past 5 p.m. when David arrived, and then we drove off to the church. The guest for the event was Bill Perkins, a powerful man of God and a noted speaker, who was supposed to preach about "The Jesus Experiment." The event started on time and went well. All the church members enjoyed it a lot. When the service was finished, Bill announced that he was willing to meet with the church members and others who needed personal prayers. Many opted to do the same, and so did I. Finally, when it was my turn, I secretly hoped to seek some answers from him. When I shared my story with him, I told him how anxiety and perpetual grief had crippled me during this divorce process and how the overwhelming thoughts of being alone had scared me. I then requested him to pray for me that I gain strength to face the next court date since the Lord had already made me escape the first date on April 20th that I dreaded the most. Then he caught hold of both my hands and said, "The Lord is able and capable. Trust Him, as far as I am concerned, I can only pray for you, but I am sure He will surely speak to you." Then he started praying persistently to seek an answer from the Lord, when suddenly the tears started dripping from my eyes, as I observed the vision of a man dressed in a long white robe holding my finger and walking me forward through the long dark road ahead of me. I was then completely choked and wept bitterly as I shared my vision with Bill. Then he said, "Do not worry! The Lord will do exactly as He has spoken and will walk you through this trial holding your hand." I then thanked him and left the church in peace as it is written in Psalm 4:8: "I will both lie down in peace, and sleep; for you alone, O Lord, make me dwell in safety."

It was pretty late when we got back home, so when I returned back to my bed that night, I could hardly sleep. The live vision of the Lord walking me through kept rewinding itself in my mind, reminding me of the verse that I had been claiming for a long in Isaiah 41:13: "For I thy God will hold thy right hand, saying unto thee, Fear not: I will help thee." The encounter with the Lord walking me through the dark road and the promise of the verse transforming into reality was a life-changing experience of the Lord's love and faithfulness towards me. Then, being filled with enormous joy that night, I slept in peace.

In a couple of days, the vision took its form when the Lord changed David's heart when he received my lawyer's letter. Then he said to me, "I have no problem with you, and you are welcome to stay here, at your home. Moreover, I will be giving you the pocket money as well for your shopping." Then, having the stability at home, I went ahead and rescheduled my interview with USCIS. The Lord straightened everything for me, and soon, I noticed a huge change in David's behavior, as he looked calm and relaxed. My prayers became more intense, and during those moments, the Spirit nudged me to say a certain thing to David. So early on a Saturday morning after he had returned from Gideon's meeting, I told him, "I know you missed all the joy of marriage, but I think you should enjoy the divorce that you desired for the remaining time that we have together." He willingly agreed the same.

The Lord's presence in this whole episode was like a real spiritual experience for me as He walked me through this journey. We both started enjoying our lives, doing all things together like going to movies, plays, suppers, playing games like Monopoly, etc., and going on outdoor trips. On Sundays, we visited the church service together, and on Wednesday evenings, we attended Bible classes. It was like a Roman holiday for us. David was too good to be true. He was kind, generous, loving, polite, and always in a happy-go-lucky mood. We both were having a blast, and it seemed like we were on a holiday spree. I saw the best side/different personality of David that I had ever seen in years. He behaved like a perfect gentleman, having all the etiquette to treat a lady well. The best moments were still to come as Christmas was on its way: the season that I loved the most since my early childhood. I believed there was magic in Christmas and that something wonderful could happen, but things were different this time, as our destiny lay in the hands of the Lord. We were both aware that it was our last Christmas together; henceforth, none of us took the initiative to celebrate the season. Soon, we observed every house in our neighborhood lit up, which simply dazzled us as we drove around town. Each decorated house depicted its own style and displayed its unique theme. Some had shimmering lights draped on fences, and some had icicle-shaped colored lights bordering their houses. Many had blue-lighted pathways, and others had yards surrounded by lighted topiary animals and flickering reindeer that kept changing their colors. Simultaneously, the street poles had also been decorated with red lanterns, golden bells, and snowflake mounts. All malls and stores also displayed their style of exuberant lighted Christmas trees, all waving their perfect magic wand of Christmas. But ours was the only house in the entire neighborhood that emitted gloom amidst these joyful surroundings. Then David suggested that we need to celebrate the season, and we went ahead with all our preparations. The Christmas tree was our family tradition, and we placed it in our living room each year. David decided to set it up, and I went ahead and decorated it with red, green, and golden tinsel garlands and hung trinkets and crystal ornaments in between it… for that was my favorite color combination. David draped the tree with colorful bulbs and fenced the whole house with flickering lights to shimmer. Finally, it was Christmas Eve, and we both attended the church service. The evening started with hymns, and the church choir sang the old Christmas carols. The lighted nativity mural with burning candles depicted the birth of Jesus in the manger, creating a perfect ambiance around the stage. Later, the lights dimmed down, and we all stood up and held candles in our hands. The whole atmosphere was pious and serene as the pastor spoke about Christmas. We worshipped the Lord in silence with our grateful hearts and then departed after greeting and having fellowship with friends. The celebration of the season continued as we both tried to connect with family and friends by sending gifts and receiving cards from their end.

Soon, time passed by, and it was December 29th, the day of our wedding anniversary. David had already left for work that morning, and I was alone at home when a wide array of emotions crossed my mind… thinking how I had struggled through the years collecting twigs like a bird to build my cozy nest, a home to live in forever after. But now, all would soon be destroyed as the tornado was on its way to leave me naked, having nothing except the shadows of empty, precious memories. The next December 29th would never come again in our lives, nor the lavish celebrations we enjoyed reliving the moments that had changed our lives. Knowing the fact that I was at the fag end of my marriage life's journey, I knew we would soon part as strangers to go our separate ways. Thinking all that in my mind, I was unable to sustain my emotions further. All I remember was that it was the saddest day of my life as I celebrated my anniversary silently and secretly with unending tears dripping from my eyes. My comforter and counselor, the Holy Spirit, reminded me that your tears are not wasted, but the Lord has already collected them. As written in Psalm 56:8, "You keep track of all my sorrows.

You have collected all my tears in your bottle. You have recorded each one in your book." Then I realized that is so true. It was then evening time, and David was back home, so we both had a quiet supper, watched a movie, and retired to our bedrooms.

The next day, David amazed me when he came back home for lunch and said, "I want you to be ready as we will be leaving tomorrow, December 31st." Then I asked him where we were going, and he replied, "It's a surprise. All I can say is that we are going to return back next year on January 2nd." I started packing to get ready for the trip, but unfortunately, I had no classy outfit for the anniversary and the New Year celebration, for I had already emptied all my closets before I would permanently leave for India.

I just had no clue where we were going or what his plan was. Since David had always been a spontaneous trip-maker, I was accustomed to those unaware trips of his that fascinated me a lot. As we drove off in the car, David said to me, "I had thought to celebrate our marriage anniversary and the New Year together since both were a day apart. So, I delayed the celebration trip." Then I thanked him for this surprise trip, as it actually worked as momentary therapy for me, to be out from the deadly clutches of my indoor suffocation. While David drove, I sat silent and cozy inside the car, watching the bejeweled brilliance of white winter, imposing an array of God's attributes. Its sheer aesthetic experience made me transcend beyond the physical realm as my eyes feasted upon the surroundings. The fields below slept snuggled within the white quilt of snow. The empty skies above glittered with majestic colors of orange, red, and shimmering gold as the rays of the sun kept peeping from behind the clouds. I felt mentally relaxed as we drove through this powdery, cloaked wintery wonderland, and I was lost in the splendor of God's glory and creation. Finally, the suspense was over as David drove his car into a posh hotel. We both checked into a room where champagne and chocolates had been laid. We both had a blast celebrating our last anniversary and New Year, enjoying our meals at lovely restaurants, and going on shopping sprees to buy the stuff that I needed to carry to India. The Lord's hand was very obvious in all this, by promising us a joyful life against all odds.

Many were amazed and shocked as I shared with them about my marriage anniversary trip. Some said, "How could you possibly enjoy and celebrate your anniversary amidst your divorce while both of your lawyers are negotiating and battling for your marital rights?" Others questioned me and asked, "How could you have enjoyed celebrating with a man who had betrayed and hurt you so badly?" Some also questioned how we could stay in peace together under the same roof. The only answer I had for all was, "Because of the Lord." For I knew in my heart that it was the Lord who had walked me through, in the midst of this adverse situation, to be an example of His resilience and grace.

Moreover, it was His responsibility to keep us joined, as it was He who put us together, as written in Mark 10:9: "Therefore what God has joined together, let no one separate." But divorce had destined us to be separated, which actually was a real controversy in itself. For Matthew 24:35 says, "Heaven and earth will pass away, but my words will never pass away."

Therefore, by gaining a deeper understanding, I knew that His Word is one hundred percent true from cover to cover. The remaining days that I had in America were consumed in prayer and petition. During the evenings, I went to Bible classes with Julie, my best friend who stood like a strong pillar beside me, and with Reena, my prayer warrior who religiously visited me to comfort and pray for me. I was blessed that the Lord put these two amazing prayer partners in my life, who jointly waited with me upon the Lord for His timely intervention.

CHAPTER 11

CELEBRATION AMIDST DIVORCE

"For thou shall be witness unto all men of what thou hast seen and heard."

– Acts 22:15

I had already entered the New Year, and it was the third week of January when I received a letter from my lawyer stating that the next court date was April 18th. I started counting the time that I had to be in the U.S. and realized I had only twelve weeks in hand. I was a bit worked up as I had lots of pending things that had to be accomplished, specifically acquiring my Citizenship before I could leave for India. But it was a very harsh wintertime, so I was unable to do my outdoor chores or report for my pending appointments. The last two weeks of January were already gone, as I had now entered into the first week of February. Although harsh winter was not my favorite season to do outdoor chores, one thing that I loved the most during those winter days was waking up late. I usually fell into deep sleep during the early morning hours and enjoyed those best moments being lost in my intense dreams. It was one of those days when I was enjoying my deep sleep, snuggled up in my soft, cozy bed when suddenly I heard my phone ring. I hesitated a lot to be awakened and avoided answering it, but it kept on ringing and ringing. Finally, I had no other option, so I stretched out my arm to lift it up and said 'Hello' in a sleepy, gruff tone and was surprised to know it was Tiara, my friend at the other end, who first said good morning to me and later apologized for disturbing me so early. She later explained to me how her other friend had ditched her at the last moment, and she had no one to manage her motel. Then she asked me if I would be kind enough to help her, as she was leaving for Washington D.C. that evening. I willingly volunteered to help her. Then she suggested I get ready soon so that she could come and fetch me before she drove out for the airport. Then, after she hung up, I felt sleepy and a bit disoriented, but still, I managed to jump out of my bed and rushed for a lovely hot shower. Soon, she was at my door and helped me pack my suitcase, and then we both drove off to the motel. When we reached the Park Motel, she explained to me everything about her hotel room keys, cash, the entry register, and how to manage money transactions. Then she settled me in the most comfortable hotel room, hugged me, and left immediately for the airport.

Then I called David to inform him that I was staying at Tiara's Park Motel to manage it as she had to leave urgently for Washington D.C. Though David was a bit surprised as to why I would stay in a motel, he said, "Okay I will join you there after work." After he hung up, I thought it was really kind of him to do that for me. Later, he arrived with lots of food and snacks that we ate, and later on, we watched TV shows until it was time for him to go. I then retired back into my hotel room, prayed, and later on dozed off to sleep. It was that night that I had a dream and I saw myself walking in the center of the road and observed a semi-truck coming straight upon me, so being scared to be killed by it, I immediately ducked and fell flat on the road, for it to pass over me. But when it was passing over me, it suddenly stopped for some reason, and I quickly rolled myself out from under it and fell far off with a jerk that awakened me. The next thing I realized was that I was still safe in my bed, thanking the Lord that it was just a dream and not a real dreadful disaster as I had thought. Then I noticed the time, and it was already 8 a.m. in the morning, so I got out of my bed, had a nice hot cup of coffee, showered, prayed, and got ready to manage the motel. The management almost kept me busy during the day, and during evening hours, David visited me religiously and brought food and snacks that we ate together until the day Tiara returned.

It was nice to be back home after this break. So when I reached home, I was surprised to see the letter sent to me from the USCIS stating that they had rescheduled my Biometrics appointment. Although I was joyful, I could not discern how they accepted my request to reschedule me after months of delay. According to the USCIS rules, Application Support Centers are instructed to provide their applicants with a 30-day time frame for rescheduling, and beyond that time frame, all petitions are denied. Yet, in my case, it looked like the Lord's intervention walked me through and beyond all restrictions of rules and regulations. David then drove me to Milwaukee for my biometrics appointment, and when I reached the office, I was given a form to fill out and asked to wait until they called me in. Later, the officer called my number, and I walked in for my fingerprints. When the officer was taking my prints, the spirit nudged me to say a certain thing to him. Then, being bold, I told him, "I don't think your machine has any problem giving you my dull prints, but it's my fingers that have no print." He got upset and told me, "I have worked here for years, and now you are trying to teach me how to do my job." I then explained to him that when I had been here for the first time, the officer repeatedly took my fingerprints but got the same results, and the prints never changed and now this is the second time that I have been called in for fingerprinting, and even if you keep on taking the prints several times more, my fingers will not change their print. He then bluntly said, "Your form does not state that it's your second Biometric test, as there is no number on it to verify that." I then asked him to call his superior to check my files, and they checked, and luckily, they found the number to put on my form. The officer then apologized and said, "Sorry, it was our mistake, but now you have the number and are all set for the Civics test and Naturalization. Then, he handed me the booklet to study for the test. I then thanked the officer and left. David was pleased to know that I was now done with the Biometrics. He then took me out for a delicious supper at India Palace, where we both enjoyed eating authentic Indian cuisine, and later drove back home. I was very happy that I was through with the Biometrics issue, but the other issue that bothered me most was the appraisal of our house, as two appraisers were scheduled to arrive at our home that day. So I sorted out my things and got ready before David walked in. Soon, the appraisers arrived, and David walked them upstairs and downstairs, into the basement, and all around the house to measure and evaluate its worth. I sat and waited, grieving in my emotional life of instability and unpredictability. Thinking that all the effort I put in for years decorating and beautifying my house to enjoy it was just a fake dream of mine that fizzled, and soon, I would be gone forever, never to return again to my home, my sweet home, as tears kept dripping down my eyes. David then walked in, and I quietly wiped my tears, pretending as if all was okay with me. The assessors then left, and we both sat down to have lunch together when David mentioned that he had planned a lavish trip for us to have a unique holiday. Finally, the day arrived, and we proceeded to Minnesota to celebrate David's birthday. David had made reservations at a posh hotel for us to stay at. For ever since we had been married, it had been our tradition to make our birthdays special. David always booked the pricy hotels and took me to the most expensive restaurants on my birthdays. But my style was different, and all that was not sufficient enough for me unless I gave David the most expensive gift to show him my love. But now all that was was history and the story of the past, as things were different this time. David had made it very clear to me in the past that gifts do not please him, and neither were they his love language. Unfortunately, he had often been upset with me on several occasions whenever I brought him Armani suits and designer stuff from the countries where I traveled. Having no idea how to please him or react this time, I preferred to step back in case I upset him with a gift. Anyway, we still enjoyed his birthday and had a blast by hanging around in different indoor hotel restaurants till late at night, enjoying music, watching movies in the hotel room, and snacking near the indoor poolside that had lovely outdoor views. Time flew fast, and then we drove back home. When we returned home, I started concentrating on the Annual Cultural Fair, which was to be held on February 28th at the University of Wisconsin. I started preparing for it, as I had lots of stuff that had to be organized and price-tagged for the coming sale. Somehow, I managed it all, and a day prior to the event, I was all set to be at the venue. David then accompanied me to help me set up the tables and stands and reserved a spot for me by hanging the poster that he had specifically designed representing 'INDIA.' The next day, we woke up early in the morning to be at the fair before the doors opened for the general public. So, as per the dress code requirement, I wore a beautiful traditional Indian outfit and gold jewelry to represent my country, and then we rushed to the venue. When we entered the hall, I observed that many vendors had already decorated their booths. David then opened up the display stands and started hanging my silk shawls, scarves, and silk tops while I started decorating my table by setting on it beautiful Bollywood jewelry, bangles, earrings, bags, and other fancy items that I had. Soon, the doors opened, and the crowds started pouring in to see the interesting broad spectrum of national displays, each reflecting its own unique individual heritage and history. The music started, and the stage lit up as singers and dancers started their performances. The food outlets were all open to serve the choicest food, and many vendors lured the passersby with free food samples to try. Most of the families admired my Indian stuff and shopped a lot.

The day was then done, and we started packing up our stuff and returned back home. I was pretty exhausted by then, so after having supper, I changed into my nightie and rushed to bed, thanking God that February was finally over. It was March 1st when I woke up, and I counted the days that I had in hand, and I had only seven weeks more. I was pleased that I had accomplished a lot, and I started my day with prayers, thanking my Lord. Then I went in for a shower and noticed that one of the gold earrings that I had worn last evening was missing from my ear. I suddenly got panicky and started searching for it in the shower in case it had fallen down, but I couldn't find it. Suddenly, a shadow of peace fell over me, and I felt in my spirit that I would surely find it because both the earrings had been intact in my ears after I had returned from the fair. After I had my shower, I searched for it all around my house and failed to find it. Days passed by, and it was on March 3rd that this incident occurred. I entered David's bathroom to weigh myself. Suddenly, something shiny on the rug caught my eye, so I grabbed it and was startled to see that it was my earring. Then I started searching for the screw but could not find it, so I walked back to my bedroom and later noticed that the screw was tightly fitted behind the earring that I had been holding in my hand. I was dazed and unable to discern how the screw got joined, and the earring reached David's bathroom, where I had never gone. Anyway, I expressed my gratitude to the Lord for getting me back what I had lost.

The next day, I narrated the whole episode to David, but he was unable to explain how the screw got fitted with the earring. Then he bid me bye and left for his outreach trip, but later called to inform me that he would be early for supper. When he got back home, we both sat down to have supper. Then David asked me if we could chat now, as he wanted to share and discuss something very important. Then, he shared with me about the encounter that he had with the Lord. While he was driving back home, he said the Lord clearly spoke to him, saying, "Have you seen the behavior in your wife recently that you felt was the cause of the problem between you?" Then David replied, "No, Lord, I have not seen any such behavior recently, and actually, ever since we filed the divorce, we had been getting along much better than any time in years of our marriage." Then David said the Lord replied, "To continue on with this divorce without any real issue between you would be because of your will to end it, and not mine." Then David told me he didn't hear anything further from the Lord, and He was gone. He said that his heart started pounding, and he immediately knew he had to stop this divorce process and planned to do that as soon as he got back home. He said that all through his journey, he kept processing the words that the Lord spoke to him and felt convicted as to why we were really having a divorce when we were getting along so well. Then, after narrating the whole episode, David said to me, "I want you to kindly withdraw this divorce, for that is not the Lord's will for us." I told him, "I will not withdraw the divorce, although I know it had never been God's will for us, for it is He who joined us together. But if you want to obey Lord to withdraw the divorce, then I suggest you better rethink, before you go ahead with it." Then he said, "That will be the first thing I will do as soon as I reach my office on Monday."

Then, early Monday morning, David called up his lawyer and told him that we had reconciled, and it had been stipulated by and between us that this action be dismissed. Thus, the Lord made David follow His commandment, as written in John 10:27: "My sheep hear my voice, and I know them, and they follow me:" Finally, the official document arrived, and it enclosed the filed copy of stipulation and an order of dismissal by the court, stating that our divorce case has been dismissed. Holding that document in my hands was like a letter of authorization from God to glorify and reveal His grandeur to one and all of what I had conquered by faith through Him.

Both Biblical records and my personal testimony attest to how God spoke into my life, as in John 16: 13-14: "But when he, the spirit of truth comes, he will guide you into all truth. He will not speak on his own; he will speak what he hears and tell you what is yet to come. He will bring glory to me by taking from what is mine and making it known to you."

It was made known to me that the roaring lion was locked in the cage and would be incapacitated to devour my marriage. That the dreaded day of divorce approaching me would be stopped, exactly as the dreaded semi-truck approaching me had stopped. Moreover, being joined back with David was like getting my lost earring back, being found and joined together. For what God joins, no one can separate. As I am writing this, I am humbled by the privilege that the Lord has given me to share my personal testimonies to glorify Him, as quoted in Acts 22:15: "For thou shall be witness unto all men of what thou hast seen and heard." I am sure when the works of the Lord are mentioned in my book; many people will be anxious to know more as to who is this God that I worshipped and waited upon and who gave me the strength to fight my battle in faith, that defied the situation I was in. That true, living Lord is Jesus, whom armies can't defeat, science can't explain, and the world cannot ignore or replace, for He is eternal and outside of time constraints with no beginning and end. So may all praise, honor, and glory be to Him - Who gave me the victory. Now it was my time to echo His praises and a time for me to celebrate, and it called for a double celebration since it was also March 14th and my birthday. David had already decorated my dining table with a lovely bouquet of red roses to wish me happy birthday, and all my friends dropped by to rejoice with me and greet me. Then we both went out for a candlelight supper, where David surprised me by planning a trip to celebrate my birthday on the coming weekend. It was Sunday, and we both left for church. The plan was to leave for the trip after the church service. We came home, loaded our carry-ons, and proceeded.

CHAPTER 12

BETRAYAL AFTER RECONCILIATION

"Good and bad do not belong together. Light and darkness cannot be shared together. How can Christ and Belial the devil have any agreement?"

– 2 Corinthians 6:14-16

Although the two of us were getting along well and enjoying all the activities of the outer world, sincerely speaking, nothing had literally changed within our inner world. David was glad that he had no more alimony issues to deal with, and likewise, I was happy to be out of the dreadful mess of divorce. Still, deep inside me, this episode had left its mark, causing a gaping wound that had yet to be dealt with. Grief does not disappear in time; as some say, "Time is a great healer." Instead, "Time is an undertaker and buries the stuff inside." That is exactly what I did; I tried to bury the stuff inside me to move on. But the irritating rash over my body spoke loud for itself and exposed its true inner self. So, I was scheduled for my visit with the doctor at the clinic. Then, after my visit with the doctor, I proceeded to the cafeteria, where David brought me a hot cup of cappuccino and started chatting and inquiring about the cause of my rash. I then told him the doctor had expressed to me that my type of rash is probably triggered by stress. Then David immediately said, "You are my only wife, and you know that I have withdrawn the divorce and have reconciled with you, and I find no reason for you to be stressed about anything now." I then told him, "Then why are you still hurting me and having relationships with your girlfriends?" He bluntly replied, "I cannot give them up since we have gone through a lot together." Then I told him, "We two have also gone through a lot together as a couple over the last eleven years." He said, "I know that, and I am trying to work on our relationship, but I need some more time to work on that." Just to hear him say that made me sick to my stomach. Thinking how low a man could fall to tell his wife that he still needs more time to work on his marriage after spending eleven years together with her as if the Lord had thrusted an unwanted project upon him. On the other hand, I observed him investing all his time and effort in building deep relationships with his girlfriends to reap the fruits of his illegitimate intimacy by putting every penny in a torn bag. A deep Satan-ordained bond that had incapacitated him to give up on them and incited him to throw away his marriage and the wife that the Lord chose for him. Then I stood up and suggested that we better leave for home as I gulped my remaining cappuccino.

When I got back home, I could hardly sleep that night and felt sad, thinking how Satan had transformed this man of God, for that was not the loving, kind man that the Lord had brought into my life. I also wondered what could have instigated him to pour out the reality of his true self and what could have been the reason for him to make an open confession about his friends now after reconciling with me.

Then I guessed that probably by doing so, he must have felt that he was clearing his conscience, but instead, by doing so, he succeeded in putting extra burdens on me by filling me with more grief and pain. Adding more fuel to the fire, or maybe by knowing that my condition was still fragile, he must have thought it was the right time for him to strike while the iron was hot. He knew that I was handicapped and would not be able to revolt after reconciliation. Since I had missed the bus, to take it or leave it, I had no other option but to accept him with his baggage as a dowry to me. Plus, it was a perfect time for him to have the best of both worlds, where everything would work well, and everyone would be happy ever after.

Instead of rebuilding the marriage after reconciliation, which requires total commitment and involvement, he tried to build his dream world of deception, where my role as a wife in his life would be just a mere title, 'WIFE.' I could not stop myself from hurting, as I had lost my equilibrium, and my body was nothing more than a battleground where there was an ongoing tussle between the truth of the reality that I was his wife and between the lie of deception that he had faked reconciliation to prove that I was his wife.

Being stressed to rebuild my life again, I was just expecting that my husband would make amends, but instead, he hit me hard to escalate my hurt. Having had no resolution, accountability, or compassion from him, I had sleepless nights, pleading before the Lord to change him. It was one of those nights when I had been awake till the wee hours, unable to catch my sleep, and I decided to leave my bed. So, I walked out of my bedroom and came downstairs. Then, as I sat on my recliner, I observed the clear blue sky, with orange and gold rays getting ready for the rising of the morning sun. It was Sunday, and it was a day for us to attend the church service. So, after a while, I went in for an early shower and later sat down to have my personal prayer time with the Lord. It was for a long time that I had been in the midst of my devotion when suddenly I heard the words, "Make straight the way of the Lord before I strike thee." I was taken aback and started wondering whether I had heard it right, what I had heard, or was it just a mere thought of mine. Not knowing what these words really meant or what to do, I started pleading before God to forgive me if I had committed any sin, but I got no response. Soon, the same words kept repeating themselves in my ears, louder and louder than ever, to make it clearer and more specific that I heard them properly. I started contending with the Lord, asking for His forgiveness to evade His wrath. When I heard a whisper, "It's not about you, tell that to David." All this came to me as a real shock, so being in a fix, I didn't know how to pass on this message to David. Then, by meditating and being convicted in my spirit of the repetitions that had occurred, I finally decided to share what the message was for David. Later, as we drove out to the church, I caught hold of David's hand and told him there was a message from the Lord for him. Then I repeated exactly the same words that I had heard, "Make straight the way of the Lord before I strike thee." I also shared with him that at first, I thought the message was for me, but it was not so when I heard the whisper that said, "It's not about you. Tell that to David." Then, as he heard me say that, he was quiet and started praying in tongues. He neither reacted nor discussed anything further, as we had already entered the church compound. All through the church service, I was perturbed and knew in my spirit that this was David's final wake-up call.

CHAPTER 13

THE FINAL WAKE-UP CALL

"And make straight paths for your feet that what is lame may not be dislocated."

– Hebrews 12:13

I don't think David took anything seriously after I conveyed the Lord's message to him, but he soon got lost in his utopia. While I, as his wife, sat silently to observe his intrinsic motivation that appeased his mind and heart. I decided not to strive for my marital rite, knowing that there is one above who observes all, as quoted in Hebrews 4:13: "And there is no creature hidden from my sight, but all things are naked and open to the eyes of Him to whom we must give account."

After I read that Word, I spoke to the Lord and said, "Yes, Lord, I know that you observe all, and nothing is hidden from you. All are accountable to you. So now it's between David and you. I am out." So, having peace in my heart, I went on to live my life.

It was exactly eight days after that Sunday when the Lord moved, and something unusual happened. It was early Tuesday morning when I was fast asleep downstairs and felt as if someone had shaken my foot. So, being awakened unawares, I was shocked to see that it was David in a crawl position, shaking my feet and asking in a slurry tone to call 911. I then got up with a jerk and caught hold of him to balance him, and it took some moments for me to realize as I was bewildered and blank seeing him in that bizarre state. Then I tried to get back to my senses and immediately called 911, pretending to be composed, just to assure David that no matter what ... our God is in control, and over and above all our problems. Then I started claiming the healing verses of the Bible, loud, while trying to get him dressed. When luckily, I noticed that the paramedics had walked in. Then they checked his blood pressure and noted all the vital signs he had experienced, and soon carried him on a transport chair to the ambulance to carry him off to the hospital. So when the ambulance was about to leave, David tried to say something to me but was unable to communicate. I was perturbed, as fear and anxiety had crept into me. Moreover, I had no clue as to what really had happened to David, as he was unable to walk or talk. I was lonely and needed help, so I called up the church prayer team to pray and decided that I would fast and pray till David recuperated fully. I was desperate to be with him, so I called the hospital staff to find out about his condition and to know the room number where he had been admitted. The nurse there informed me that he had been admitted to the emergency room, and the doctors were working on him and had decided to take different tests to diagnose his problem. After learning that, I packed my stuff and left home for an overnight stay at the hospital. When I reached the hospital, I was shocked to find out that the doctors had now shifted David to the Intensive Care Unit. Knowing that, I was traumatized thinking that only patients who are in critical condition are admitted to ICU. I was completely stressed out, as I was not mentally or emotionally prepared for that. Then, trusting, praising, and focusing on my awesome Lord to cope with the situation, I slowly walked up to David's room and found him resting on his bed. Then I said 'Hi' to him, and he smiled as I sat next to him and chatted while the nurses kept coming in and out, monitoring him. Finally, they pulled the curtains and requested me to leave the room. I then left the room and waited in the lounge till late at night, until I was completely exhausted. I decided to return to David's room to keep watch on him all through the night. Although I felt uncomfortable and sleepless, I pursued praying and pleading before the Lord for His mercy. Suddenly, I felt a spell of peace dawn on me as my whole body resonated with the thought that this probably was the Lord's plan to refine David by striking him with the stroke to chasten him. I knew that God's statutes hinge on our obedience, mostly when He makes us walk through the fiery path of trials by putting us out of one test and into another. I thought this was probably God's way to refine him, just as the goldsmith refines his gold through the flames of fire. By the next day, my covenant Lord had done His job, and by afternoon, the doctor released David from the hospital. After he returned back home, we rejoiced, thanking our gracious God. By the next evening, David felt good, so I thought it was the best time for me to hear his story as to what had really happened to him. Then he sat down to narrate it to me and said, "I woke up at 5:15 a.m., as usual, to attend the Tuesday Bible study at the church. As I was getting ready, I could feel that something was wrong with my body. My left arm did not seem to be working in a normal manner. I felt I did not have full control of it, and soon, I felt the same thing happening to my legs. My thought was that I would not be able to continue to stand on my own, so I sat down on the floor. I had never had an experience like this in my life, but I knew that what was happening to me were symptoms of a stroke. The thought came to me that people die from symptoms like these. So rather than to dwell on those thoughts, I called out to my Lord Jesus and claimed healing and protection. As I sat on the floor calling out to Jesus, the symptoms grew worse. I was having great difficulty controlling my arms and hands as if I was partially paralyzed. I knew I needed help, so I crawled over to my dresser and was able to reach my phone lying on top of it. I then pushed the button to call you, but the phone rang several times and went on to a voice mail. I knew you were fast asleep and must have not heard the phone ringing. Knowing I needed help, I then crawled to the stairs and slowly scooted down the stairs, one foot at a time. When I reached the bottom of the stairs, I crawled up to your recliner where you were sleeping, and shook you by the leg to wake you up. I needed help and then asked you to call 911. After you called 911, my symptoms continued to deteriorate more. Not only had I lost control of my limbs, but I felt my face numb and my words slurred, making it very difficult for me to tell you what was happening to me. I was mentally crying out to Jesus while fighting the urge to panic. I knew my fate was in God's hands, and I was grateful to God that the EMTs had arrived within minutes at our place. Soon after they took me to the hospital, I was immediately admitted by them into the emergency room, where a heart monitor was connected to me, and my blood pressure was measured every ten minutes. Then, several doctors and nurses came in and spoke to me, asking many questions. By this time, the symptoms that had dawned on me a couple of times earlier had left me. So it was easy for me to communicate with the doctors. I spent the rest of the morning and afternoon having many tests done, including a cardiac ultrasound scan, x-rays, and an MRI. By evening, they moved me to the intensive care unit, and I was told I had to be on full-time overnight monitoring because of the strong medication they were using on me. By late evening, when you arrived, my blood pressure was down once again in the normal range as they had changed my IV medication to oral pills to control my blood pressure. The next morning, when you were at the pharmacy, a team of doctors arrived and gave me the good news that all tests were clear, and none of these tests showed any damage to my heart or brain. Moreover, they said that the final result of the diagnosis showed that it was probably the high blood pressure that had triggered the paralytic attack." After David narrated this to me, he also told me about the weird dream that his twin brother had about him that very same day. David said, "My brother saw that I was dead, and he was at my funeral, and all this was to me, like double confirmation, that the Lord had spared my life in His mercy. Now, I truly believe that this was a final wake-up call for my spiritual walk."

After I heard all of that from David, I told him. "The meaning of a Spiritual walk is to live your life as a Christian… the one who desires to have the essence of the law fulfilled in his Christian life., as mentioned in Romans 8:1." "There is therefore now no condemnation to those who are in Christ Jesus, who do not walk according to the flesh, but according to the Spirit." Then David said, "So true! I do agree with that." But, in spite of all that, he soon forgot about everything and went on to live his usual life of addiction by hiding his cell from me and communicating secretly with his friends. Well! Then I called upon the Lord and said, "Lord, now it is between You and David. You are the Mighty One to judge, and it's Your department. I know that You will judge David in Your righteousness. Thanks for setting me free. Now, I will just chill out and wait to rejoice in the outcome of Your glory and grandeur."

CHAPTER 14

MOCKING GOD BY FAKE VOWS

They prove the point of the proverbs, "A dog goes back to its own vomit," and, "A scrubbed-up pig heads for the mud."

– 2 Peter 2:22 MSG

Then, knowing that David was back in square one, I decided to quiet down in the lush pastures of the Lord's peace to make my humble requests known to Him. The Bible verse says, "Be anxious for nothing; but in everything by prayer and supplication with Thanksgiving, let your requests be made known to God." Philippians 4:6. I then relaxed calmly under the shadow of His wings, awaiting to see the splendor of His saving grace.

A couple of weeks had passed by, and it was Sunday morning, when David had already left early for his usual hour of prayer at the church. I was at home praying, waiting for him to come and fetch me. Soon, he arrived, and we drove off to the church. It was during that church service that David quietly handed over a note to me that stated, "The Lord did something amazing and deep down within me today to restore me to the position where I would reflect His glory and character through my life." So, as I read the note, I was flabbergasted that the Lord had answered my requests so swiftly. Then I smiled at David and said, "Now I can hardly wait to hear your story." Then, after church, when we reached back home and had finished eating our lunch, David sat down to narrate the whole story to me about his encounter with the Lord and said, "When I got up early this morning, I was in high spirits, feeling great and physically fit as a fiddle, feeling grateful in my heart for the Lord's mercy. I was also excited to reach church soon to praise God for bringing me back home safe and sound from the hospital. When I entered the church, I heard the worship songs echoing loudly in the auditorium, and then I walked and sat down far in the last row. Feeling much joy for that blessed day, I folded my hands and then knelt down, humbling myself, praying, praising, and glorifying the Lord for being such a great and merciful God. So, being focused, I kept meditating on the oasis of His serenity and grace when something unusual happened to me. Suddenly, in the midst of my fervent prayer, I was able to sense in my spirit a clear vision of His holiness, pure and pious before me. Then, being lost in His Majesty's glory, I noticed myself being seated under a direct spotlight instantly, which made me look through my true inner self as if some X-ray eyes had been given to me.

Soon, the secret pockets and the sin compartments of my life started opening up just like a world map automatically unfolding itself. I could clearly see exactly as the Lord had observed those compartments, which appeared to me like dirty images of festering, bubbling pools of pus and vial liquid. Stinking and ugly a sight as one could ever imagine. Seeing my own spiritual condition being so deplorable, I loathed myself, and suddenly, the spirit of repentance overwhelmed me, feeling the debt of my sin.

Then, being guilty, I fell on my face before my righteous and holy God and begged Him for forgiveness for my rebellion against Him. I also petitioned Him to cleanse these filthy pockets out of my life, sobbing and shedding tears of repentance, which lasted for almost an hour-long session of prayer.

I then felt that the Lord had washed me clean after the strong repentance that I had gone through, which filled me with peace and joy, knowing that my life had been changed forever. I had a strong sense that He would now enable me to make every other change that I needed to accomplish. Then, I invited Him to be the Sole Master of every area of my life and vowed never to rebel against Him from that moment and day forward. I also promised Him that from now on, I would be open and transparent to Him and my wife, and I have decided to walk in his ways that would bring peace, joy, and blessings into our lives."

After David had finished narrating his testimony to me, he said, "I am very happy today. Now, let's go out and do something interesting." But it was a very odd time for that. So we just drove out and later entered the Starbucks coffee shop to have our favorite cappuccinos. Then, as we sat down and got settled, chatting and sipping our coffee, I asked David, "Do you know how much God loves you?" He replied, "Yes! Surely I know that God loves me, but He did not love me too much to leave me as I was; that's why he chastened me." Then I said, "Now, I can compare you with the apostle Paul, whom the Lord had chastened to become a preacher, from a persecutor." As quoted in Proverbs 3:12: "For whom the Lord loves He corrects, just as a father the son in whom he delights."

Then David laughed out loud and said, "I know he chastened me like Paul, but now I need to make every other change that He wants me to accomplish." But what he really meant by every other change, I was not quite sure of, which came to light when suddenly I heard a sound that was none other than the signal of David's incoming message. I told him, "Look! There is a message for you," and without any hesitation, he immediately took his phone out of his pocket and read the message. I then asked him if I could have his phone, and when I read his message, I noticed the call was from some company. So, I asked David how this number is registered in a company's name. Then David frankly told me that he had fed his girlfriend's number in a company's name to hide her identity from me and that he was now sick of doing all those hanky-panky things and just wanted to get out of this rut to be done with them. As David opened up to spill the beans, I was stunned and speechless, thinking how the Lord had reversed the whole situation as quoted in Luke 8:17: "For there is nothing secret that will not be revealed, nor anything hidden that will not be known and come to light."

Simultaneously, I was also amazed at how the Lord had loosened David's chains to get him released from the grip of Satan and had given him the power to come out in the open. So, his very secretive life that had disgusted me, visa-versa, now disgusts him to the extent that he wants to be done with it. I then suggested to David that the best way to get out of this rut would be if he changed both his email address and phone number, and he agreed to do the same. So, after we had finished our coffee, we both went to the store from where we had purchased our iPhones and asked the manager to get us a new number. The manager said, "It's a long process and will take time." So we left the store and drove back home. After having my supper, I retired to my bed and thanked the Lord for his Divine intervention that convicted David to confess, repent, and forsake his rebellion, as quoted in Proverbs 28:13: "He that covers his sins will not prosper, but whoever confesses and forsakes them will have mercy."

The next morning, David left his phone back home before leaving for his Bible class. I picked up his phone and noticed two more messages from his other girlfriends. But I overlooked all that, as I was not interested in delving into his junk. I was sure that David had decided not to associate with them in the future. I then contacted the telephone company directly and asked the lady concerned to change my husband's cell number. Moreover, I explained to her how the continuous anonymous callers had been harassing him, so she finally agreed to cancel David's old number and allotted me a brand-new number for him without any cost.

Later, when David was back home, I handed him his phone and congratulated him on his new number, trusting that from now on, he would start his life on a new, clean slate. Knowing that his intention was good, all through this process of pain caused by the violation of marriage trust, I stood beside David like a strong pillar, letting aside my emotions and trying to calm my nerves so I don't get wild to confront him about his lies and betrayal. Instead, I focused on him so that he could accomplish all the changes he desired to make and pay his vows to the Lord. Moreover, unlike any other woman who has zero tolerance for infidelity, I walked according to my Indian values and morals to keep up my grace and dignity without accusing him or even pinpointing his flaws. As quoted in Proverbs 19:11, "Sensible people control their temper; they earn respect for overlooking wrongs."

But unfortunately, I failed to earn respect, as David took advantage of my grace.

By not confronting and controlling my temper, he got the impression that I had no guts, and by not pinpointing his flaws, he conceived that I was too scared, thinking that I was a sissy and not the type to create havoc. Plus, knowing that I was weak and all alone in America boosted him to imagine that he was the master of his own will, who had the reins in his own hands, who did what he wanted without any repercussions, who can still do what he wants to whom he wants. Being open and transparent before God and me, he felt like he had won a battle and started living his life like one of those lonely, unconcerned, uncaring people answerable to none and to whom rules don't apply, nor responsibility, accountability, or liability for repercussions.

Feeling free that he was now answerable to no one fed his ego with joy. Moreover, having the peace that his confession had cleansed him, he went on to live his life on his own terms, being back to square one and busy at work during the daytime and with his iPad and television during the evenings. All that was heartbreaking for me as I observed him nullifying the Lord's plan that he had for our marriage. The disrespect I had tolerated but mocking

God was unacceptable to me. I was worried and didn't want David to suffer again, as the Lord had already struck both of his legs to make him realize that it was his final wake-up call as written in Hebrews 12:13 : "And make straight paths for your feet so that what is lame may not be dislocated, but rather healed."

But instead of making a straight path for his feet, he walked in his own ways contrary to Christian beliefs, as written in 1 Psalm 107:11

"They rebelled against the words of God, scorning the counsel of the Most High."

The fruit of their rebellion was none other than Mocking God, and being a woman of God, I was not ready to give up on David. So, I started my spiritual warfare to save him from the clutches of the wicked one through prayers and petitions, for I could clearly see how Satan operated through him as David completely neglected me and gave me the silent treatment that incapacitated him to converse with me. But that was not the man I had married, who was cruel and mean, and as days, weeks, and months passed by, David kept pace with them and completely isolated himself from me to widen the rift between us. For it is written in Proverbs 18:1, "A man who isolates himself seeks his own desire; he rages against all wise judgment."

Finally, he hid himself behind a thick, impenetrable wall, creating a strained, toxic atmosphere in the house that suffocated me. He made it impossible for me to deal with him, even in my normal day-to-day life. By doing all that, he succeeded in making me a recipient of psychological distress, which impacted the level of my functioning. I had no visa to travel to India nor a miracle pill to heal myself. So I tried my best to tolerate his undeserving, undesirable, boorish acts, being choked that started a war within me. I was completely stressed out and on the verge of an emotional breakdown, thinking how could any strong man of God well versed in Biblical literature and knowing about the repercussions of disobedience of the commandments of the Lord behave like that? My heart just broke, and I was unable to change David as he kept filling the marriage reservoir with all the toxins. As William Shakespeare said, "The grief that does not speak whispers the over-fraught heart and bids it to break." So it was on July 29, that I finally broke down and developed severe chest pain that made it impossible for me to move my back and left arm. Then I called up my friend and explained my condition to her, and she got very upset with me and forced me to see the doctor immediately. Then, when David returned home for lunch, he drove me straight to the emergency care unit of the hospital. The doctor checked me and said, "We will have to do all the tests to check if the pain was caused by any heart abnormality." So, they did all the Lab tests, CT scan, chest X-ray, and then put me on a very tough Exercise

Stress Echocardiogram and then took me by wheelchair to get my Electrocardiography done. Then, as I sat alone in pain outside the operation theatre, the whole ambiance around me made me very nervous. I started calling upon the name of the Lord to help me walk through this next test of trial. Thus, by faith, I entered the operating theatre, trusting Jesus. For "FAITH" expects from God what is beyond all expectation. By early the next morning, when the doctor arrived in my room, he brought my report in and said, "Your heart is in perfect condition, and the cause of the pain was probably due to severe stress." He gave me permission to be released from the hospital, so when I got back home, I humbled myself, thanking God for putting me through these tests that assured and taught me a lot, as written in Psalms 119:50: "This is my comfort in my affliction, for Your word has given me life."

CHAPTER 15

THE SHAME GAME

"They are like wild waves of the sea, churning up the foam of their shameful deeds. They are like wandering stars, doomed forever to blackest darkness."

– Jude 1:13

Thus, through His word, I finally got the assurance from Psalm 119:71: "It is good for me that I have been afflicted, that I may learn your statutes." Then I realized that it was the Lord's wonderful plan to allow me to go through these trials, to give me advanced training and the ability to deal with my isolation to come out as a winner, which changed my whole perspective towards life after I returned home from the hospital... thinking, what if I had died in the operation theatre, then what....? What is "leftover" after life is over? I then realized that death is the end of life, but I had died being alive by waking up each day with two choices: "Which bridge to cross and which bridge to burn?" Just being drowned down in the past hurt each day without even looking up to the Lord, who already had something better in store for me. To lift me up from hopeless existence to achieve consequential victory, and that something more of significance inspired me that I need to focus on the Lord and not on trivial, insignificant things that had made me miserable. Moreover, I realized that I had also jumbled up my personality from a Gospel singer, who was destined to glorify God, to be a housewife to serve David by entering deeper into a housewife mode, forgetting that it was just a role and not my real self, who wanted to serve the Lord. All that assured me that my priorities had changed. Since I had neglected my ministry to be with David, managing and doing the household chores that would please him. Unfortunately, all that did not work, and neither was it David's love language. Henceforth, I failed to fit into the image of his fantasy world's ideal bride, for which I don't blame him either because everyone dreams. But only fools expect dreams to become a reality, and the reality of my life was that I was myself a fool, thinking David is my husband, my better half. But sorry to say, he just wasn't mine. Luckily, I had One, Who was mine, better and above all, Who loved me unconditionally, Whom I also trusted, and Who would never leave me in a lurch nor forsake me. Thus, I kept pleading with Him, "Make haste to help me so that I may be free to serve and rejoice in you." But still, He never answered nor moved. So, being a strong woman of faith, I knew my Lord was never silent. He is constantly at work, doing something for you, as quoted in Jeremiah 29:11, "For I know the plans I have for you," declares the Lord, "Plans to prosper you and not to harm you, plans to give you hope and future." I knew my potential existed in the totality of all the plans and possibilities the Lord had for my life. He moved according to His plan and made it possible for my OCI forms to be accepted by the OCI department for verification with my U.S. Passport so that I could obtain a permanent visa to travel to India.

All through this time, I noticed David enjoying his independence by taking part in different activities and making plans without me, by doing everything himself. By leaving for fake maximum outreach official trips, solo trips to visit his family, solo trips for conventions, solo trips for Gideon's suppers, banquets, and trips to the golf club for practice. Earlier in our relationship, it was different, as he had never taken a single trip without me and had always asked me to join him. I wondered at him, as he kept abusing me in multiple ways by leaving me alone and secluded at home for weeks. But wounds heal faster when you do not touch them and leave them alone. Still, I kept touching my raw wounds as I kept writing the story of my life. There were moments when I could neither write nor concentrate and would sit in my solitude, shedding tears and asking the Lord to give me strength and wisdom to live this solitary, married life. It was one of those evenings when I was reading my Bible when one of the verses stood out to me in Proverbs 19:8: "The one who gets wisdom loves life, and one who cherishes understanding will soon prosper." That was the moment I realized that I had failed to cherish my 'LIFE' because I lacked wisdom and had no gratitude towards the Lord. For the priceless gift that He had blessed me with. The life that He gave me is to touch people's lives, serve Him, achieve goals, and prosper by being happy in Him. Then, I asked for forgiveness from the Lord and waited patiently for him to open new doors for me so that I could get involved in ministry work. Soon, in a couple of days, I got a phone call from the editor of a popular magazine in Wisconsin, saying that they had heard a lot about me and wanted to feature my article in their "You Magazine" in the most prestigious section page, "The Woman You Should Know." They asked me if I could fill in their Resume Form to get some feedback about my qualifications, family, achievements, talents, choices, and future plans that I desired to accomplish in life, plus one of my best photographs to print above my article. I did what was needed, and they sent me a thank you letter informing me that I would be featured in the month of August in their next edition. But the Lord did not stop there and soon opened more doors for me. It was on Saturday afternoon when David was out in the yard mowing the lawn when someone knocked on my door. So I peeped through the door and asked the gentleman what he wanted, and he said, "I have come to meet Kadambari, I am sure that is you." I smiled at him and said, "You are welcome. Please come in and be seated; I will join you in a few moments." Then I went in to see my face in the mirror, combed my hair, applied some blush on to look pleasant-able, and walked back into the living room, where he was seated. Then he stood up to shake hands with me and said, "I am Mr. Dan, the organizer of the India Mission Joy." Then we both sat down to chat and during that long conversation that we had, he mentioned that he was organizing "The India Festival" in Wisconsin on a very large scale to honor Mother Teresa and had come here to invite me to be their guest artist at their function. He needed my consent so that he could send me an official letter for approval. Then I told Mr. Dan that Mother Teresa is my hero, whom I have admired all my life for the amazing work she did. It would be my pleasure to join you for her celebration. Then, after we had our coffee, Mr. Dan thanked me and left, taking some of my fliers and photographs to print posters and fliers for the India Festival publicity campaign. So, within a few days, my fliers were pasted all across the Wisconsin area, and the India Festival was broadcast on local radio stations and through TV advertisements for promotion. Soon, time passed by, and I started getting phone calls from my friends that they had read my write-ups in the News Herald, Hub City Times, and in several other Wisconsin newspapers. Then Mr. Dan sent me some of the festival posters and fliers, requesting to get them distributed through my Indian friends in Minneapolis, as I had told him I would be leaving soon for my family reunion, which was coming up on August 11.

Then I got busy preparing for the reunion as I had to pack my clothes and shop for the reunion goodies, plus the other things that we both needed there. Finally, it was time to leave, and we drove off to Minneapolis and stayed at a lovely hotel surrounded by restaurants and a park. The staff there welcomed us and allotted us the best suite, which was attached to a complimentary conference room. So we walked in and soon got settled in the suite to take a little nap, and by evening, we freshened up and left to join other family members who had arrived. Now, when all the members had gathered at the reception, we left for supper at a nearby Italian restaurant and then decided to meet back at the conference room to set the tables with goodies and snacks that each one of us had brought for our late-night snack. So by the time, we all got back after supper, the staff had already pasted my posters and write-ups in our private conference room, at the hotel's reception area, and at the swimming pool area, where the hotel management also laid the morning breakfast for all the hotel guests.

By 9:30, all latecomers had arrived, and they also joined us at the conference room, which soon got jam-packed. We all sat down around different tables to play the choice of game that each one preferred. Some sat down to have coffee, some sipped wine, some watched videos, and some were back in the swimming pool playing games. Plus, some elders sat down to chat, sharing their past stories and jokes till late. So we all enjoyed and had a lot of fun that night. By the next morning, after having breakfast together, everyone had the option to do what each desired, and the same routine continued the next day. Finally, the night before returning home, we had a complimentary pizza party and a huge cake to celebrate David's relative's birthday. Then, by the next morning, after breakfast, we all prayed as it was Sunday, a time for church service, and then departed, bidding adieu to all. The trip back home was great, and the weather was lovely. While David drove, I sat quietly, sorting out the things in my mind that I had to accomplish. So when I reached back home I unpacked all my stuff, and now my priority was to prepare for my upcoming performance on August 27, which was approaching fast. I had to check out what sort of prearrangements had been done for me at the auditorium. Since I had no orchestra or band to sing with and had to perform with pre-recorded music. I needed a sound system that could synchronize my voice with the music track while I performed live. However, for all that arrangement, I had not yet received any feedback from my organizer. So, I called the high school, the venue for the festival, to contact the person in charge there, and was shocked to find out that the auditorium had no sound engineer nor any equipment that a performing artiste needed, but the usual equipment and mike, to cater to the school needs for lectures and seminars. All that was too frustrating for me to hear, as I was not ready to ruin the image that I had built serving the Lord for years.

All that made me morose and withdrawn, and I sat down to figure out other options when the other organizer, Father Peter, called me up. Then I asked him about the sound arrangement, and he said, "Mr. Dan is handling all that; I have no idea about it." Then he asked if I could set up a stall at the India Festival to display my Indian artifacts, but I declined, explaining to him that it would be practically impossible for me to handle and manage my stall on the day of my performance and I apologized, saying sorry to him. But again, the next morning, Father Peter called me up to inform me that four of his church members had volunteered to help me and would be at my place by six in the evening to help and handle everything. Plus, they have also agreed to set up my stall and manage it throughout the festival day. So, by evening, all the ladies arrived at my place, and we all sat down, sorting different artifacts, putting on price tags, and making notes of all the items that I had for sale. But all that was very time-consuming and frustrating for me, as my priority was just to get set for my performance.

After the ladies left, I asked David if he had charged the battery for my camera, which I had left on his table three days earlier, and he bluntly replied and said, "I do not know how to charge it." So, hearing his rude, rebellious answer, I started working on it and somehow managed to charge the battery for my friend, who wanted to videotape the India Festival.

Then, when I retired to bed, I blamed myself for expecting something from David, a God fearing man known as my husband, and decided that I needed to grow up to be on my own. So, by the afternoon of the next day, I left on my own for my doctor's appointment at the hospital. As I walked through the corridor to the reception area, I noticed the August edition of the "You Magazine" lying there. Then being excited I picked it up and read my coverage, and then I took it along to share it with David. But when I told him that I had been featured in this magazine, he did not react to it at all, nor asked for the magazine to read my article- not a sentence. I left it on his table and asked him to share it with his office colleagues. Then he bluntly said, "Why would I do that? I am not sitting here to promote you. This is my office, and I am not so friendly with my staff." After hearing his mean statement, I left and proceeded further to visit my doctor.

After my visit with the doctor was over, a friend of mine drove me to the auditorium, where I met a couple of youngsters setting up the stage for the festival. I asked them if they knew any guy who could monitor my sound, so they all sat down to help me, making calls to different friends who were musicians and finally called over a young amateur guy who volunteered to bring in a small machine that he had at home to get my voice synchronized with my music track. I rehearsed for an hour or so, singing along with my music track, and finally, he succeeded in getting some results. He then volunteered to monitor my sound. I returned back home thanking God for making all things work for me, as quoted in Romans 8:28: "And we know that all things work together for good to those who love God, to those who are called according to His purpose."

Finally, the next morning was the day of the India Festival, and I asked David if he would like to attend the same, and he said, "Yes." So, by evening, when I had got all dressed and ready, we left for the auditorium. As I walked into the venue, I noticed lots of decorated stalls around and the Indian buffet tables getting cleared up. I proceeded towards the auditorium and noticed people walking fast and entering to occupy the best seats. Within minutes, the show started with a couple of speeches, and then other performers took over the stage, performing their solo items. Finally, after a couple of items, Father Peter gave my introductory speech and invited me to come on stage. After thanking him and my video presentation, I started my performance, by singing my popular superhit Gospel songs to praise and glorify God, and immediately I received a thundering applause from the audience, which was like an assurance for me from the Lord, that only He can turn a mess into a message, a test into a testimony, a trial into triumph, and a victim into victory. I stayed back to watch other dance items performed by other solo artists and dance groups. Finally, the show was over, and as I walked out, many people stood up to shake hands with me. Others stopped by my stall to compliment me, to buy my CDs, and some clicked selfies with me. But David turned his back and stood far from me. Later, he loaded the artifacts in the car, and as we drove back home, he said, "The members of our church who were chatting with me said that you did a good job, like a pro, and you knew how to capture your audience well, and yours was the best performance for that night." So, I thanked him for sharing that information with me. The next morning at church, the members repeated the same words to me, and I told them all Glory belongs to the Lord.

After returning from the church and having a good night's sleep, by the next day, I felt really relieved, as I was done with all my liabilities. I started my search for the best deals to book my ticket to Mumbai, India. I kept browsing different sites because I was not sure when the Lord wanted me to leave, so I just kept gathering information. Suddenly, I heard a knock at my door, and when I walked up to the door, I saw the envelope lying on my floor. I picked it up, and to my surprise, it was my U.S. passport with an OCI card attached to it. A lifetime visa to travel hassle-free. I was thrilled, and my joy knew no bounds to fly away far forever. Moreover, I was done and tired of keeping the fake front before others after continuously fighting the demons behind the scenes of my life. David never stopped, and repeatedly kept on emotionally abusing me in an insidious, elusive way time and time again, and did not even spare the night when I returned back from the hospital, which had hit me hard. All this happened when we both were watching the PBS channel. When a Muslim man in Saudi Arabia caught hold of his wife, dropped her on the floor, and chopped off her neck, immediately after watching that cruel act, David said to me, "Do you want to go to Saudi?" I replied, "Yes, that would be a nice experience for me to watch how men kill their wives." But he kept quiet and did not speak a single word. All that came across to me was that he wanted me to experience the same. It was at that very moment I had a tingling feeling in the pit of my stomach, suggesting that I needed to get out and run as fast as I could. As quoted in Proverbs 12:18, "There is one who speaks like the piercing of a sword, but the tongue of the wise promotes health."

If David had behaved with me wisely, he would have promoted my health, but instead, he deteriorated my health by repeatedly piercing me with harsh words that Satan cunningly kept prompting him to speak. Then I cried out loud before the Lord, questioning Him, "Don't You see how he hurts me? How long will you allow me to be hurt, how long, Lord? Give ear to my supplications, and answer me in Your righteousness." But as usual, the Lord was silent. I was persistent and kept pleading with Him to answer me swiftly. Finally, I got His answer, consoling me, "It's not you that I want to hurt. But it is he whom I have hurt by depriving him to love and cherish his wife till the score is settled." Then I was at ease, having the assurance from the Lord that hurt and pain were really not meant for me, nor my cup of tea as I had presumed. Out of the deepest pain, I got the strongest conviction of the presence of the Lord's love for me. Then I prayed to the Lord for mercy upon David.

Thus, the Mighty Lord, Who chose to put us together, had now chosen to withdraw me. As promised in Psalm 107:28-30 "Then they cry out to the Lord in their trouble, and He brings them out of their distress. He calms the storm so that the waves are still. Then they are glad because they are quiet, so He guides them to their desired haven."

The Lord fulfilled His Word by guiding me to be at the desired haven, and this happened as He spoke into my life on a Saturday afternoon while I was busy writing my book. All of a sudden, I started writing what I heard was being dictated to me and not what I had been writing in continuation of my chapter. I do not really remember how that happened to me, as I was in a trance, carried away in a flow, and kept writing what was being prompted to me, as follows, "Listen, my child, now enter my rest and enter my peace. Listen, obey, and follow, for I have a mission for you when you leave for India. I want you to go to the poor and needy, to serve them, and preach the Gospel. Then shall I put you on the next mission that your heart desires? Do not hesitate or be confounded, for I, thy God, is in control. Do as I say that you may succeed and prosper in all that you do." Then I asked the Lord and said, "Give me the time and date when I should leave." He replied, "Your time and date are perfect." Then I said, "Lord bless me." He said, "Blessings, I bless you. Your cup shall run over." After I was done writing, I was not aware of what I wrote and why I wrote, so I started reading it, and then realized that it was the Lord Who had entrusted me to serve the poor, by His command similarly as written in Titus 1:3 "At the right time he revealed his message through the proclamation that was entrusted to me by the command of God our savior." Moreover, He wanted to withdraw me out of all tribulations to enter His peace as also promised in John 16:33: "These things I have spoken to you, that in Me you may have peace. In the world you will have tribulation: but be of good cheer, I have overcome the world."

Being full of good cheer, I immediately booked my ticket to leave on September 27th, but being refrained by the Spirit, I did not confirm the date of my return ticket back to the U.S. Then I started sorting out all my wardrobes to find out what I should carry that is light, so that I could stuff more into my suitcases. Moreover, my pending annual check-ups at the hospital were also done. I got busy shopping for gift items for my friends and family. Finally, my lucky September 27th, arrived and we were all set to leave for Chicago O'Hare International Airport. Then, before I could leave my home, David started loading all my stuff into the car. I then removed my two big portraits from our living room so that I leave no trace of mine behind in the house. When we reached Airport Terminal 2, David helped me to stroll in my luggage near the counter and left to park the car, and by the time he was back, I had already checked in my luggage and had received my boarding pass. We both sat down silently as strangers and waited for security check-up time. I asked David to leave before it would be rush time for him to drive back to Wisconsin. But he waited until I walked out clear after my security check, waving goodbye to me from a distance. Later on, I just walked ahead to board my much-awaited flight to freedom, strolling my suitcase with self-dignity. When the flight took off, I sat silently and prayed, and after having my meal, I dozed off, entering into His rest until it was time for my flight to land at The Chhatrapati Shivaji Maharaj International Airport Mumbai, India.

CHAPTER 16

GOD WITHDRAWS ME OUT

"The way of life winds upward for the wise, that he may turn away from hell below."

– Proverbs 15:24 NKJV

When I landed in Mumbai, I was completely at ease since the Lord had orchestrated this transition for me, saying 'Count it all for joy when you fall into various trials, knowing that the testing of your faith produces patience." God always meets us where we are and takes us where He wants us to go. So being patient, I chose not to regret the things of the past but chose to thank God for the goodness that He allowed me to walk through these fiery trials. For God never allows pain without a purpose. Neither does he allow any circumstance or person to afflict you unless He has that affliction for our good. Likewise, the affliction inflicted upon me was for my ultimate good, which taught me how to be wise through the above Bible verse that says,

"The way of life winds upward for the wise, that he may turn away from hell below."

But I did not turn or walk away from the U.S. to prove my animosity or self-worth to David, but to acknowledge myself, my worth, knowing who I was in Christ, a child of God, the daughter of the Kings of King, and an heir of His promise. Moreover, I knew it was my time to walk away. As the saying goes, when to walk away needs 'WISDOM being able to walk away needs 'COURAGE,' and walking away in grace needs 'DIGNITY.' I opted to walk away in dignity when David stepped out of his marriage vows and repeatedly kept saying, "I have a new strategy, but I will tell you when the right time comes." Instead of speaking out his strategy verbally, he practically played it out according to his plan for his bright future. He crossed all boundaries through his actions and hurtful statements to ultimately achieve his goal. But all that Satan did to hurt and harm me, the Lord transformed it in my favor. For if David had loved me, it would have been too difficult for me to leave him and walk out. But, all the hurt and pain he caused me turned out to be a blessing in disguise and gave me the power to take responsibility for my own life and to disempower him from the privilege he had to steer my life's carriage. So, I started my own life's journey partnering with the Lord, realizing that it was a foolish fault of my expectation that had snatched my joy. I took the first major step to take responsibility and ownership of my "emotions" by "deleting" all my inborn emotional attachments, longings, dreams from my heart, and foolish expectations from my so called husband. Acknowledging to myself that my dream of living happily ever after marriage was just a wild wish of mine. My longing to share my sunset years with someone special, my stupid expectation, and the one who would cherish my company, chatting and relaxing on a recliner… rubbish. That helped me to reconcile with the reality of my marriage in a stride. Moreover, I knew the Lord definitely had a purpose for my pain, as He had for most of the Biblical characters. Moses experienced pain while wandering in the wilderness for forty years but was finally blessed when he reached the Promised Land. Job, having lost everything, his sons, cattle, wealth, and health, was later blessed in double measure. Joseph, after being thrown in a ditch and sold by his brothers in slavery and imprisoned on false slander, was later blessed to attain a high position next to King Pharaoh. So also, when Abraham was asked to leave his own country by the Lord at the old age of seventy five, he was abundantly blessed in double measure, as written in Genesis 12:1:

“

"Get out of your country
From your family
And from your father's house.
To the land which I will show you.
I will make you a great nation.
I will bless you,
And make your name great;
And so you shall be a blessing."

”

Thus, Abram was blessed and received his inheritance from the Wadi of Egypt to the great river, Euphrates. Genesis 15:18.

By faith, I also knew the Lord had a purpose for me to leave my country, the U.S. when He spoke to me and said, "Blessings, I will bless you. Your cup shall run over." Exactly as it is written in Isaiah 54:6-7 "The Lord will call you back as if you were a wife deserted and distressed in spirit – a wife who married young, only to be rejected," says your God. "For a brief moment, I abandoned you, but with deep compassion, I will bring you back." The Lord brought me back with deep compassion and blessed me by providing me with a beautiful three-bedroom apartment in a posh area opposite the seashore. A perfect time for Him to help me transition from hell to happiness and from sorrow to joy as promised in John 16:22 "Therefore now you have sorrow, but I will see you again and your heart will rejoice, and your joy no one will take from you."

That was so true; the Lord had already withdrawn me away so that no one could snatch my joy. Thus, I was all set and started the process of my transition to revisit and relive that very part of my life that I had abandoned, crushed, and silenced. The enthusiastic, happy-go-lucky gal that I was, traveling around the world spreading the gospel, knowing fully well that the purpose of my life was to be happy in the Lord. Life is to live in the present and enjoy every moment, for that is all our portion in vain life, without any promise for tomorrow.

But still, during those moments of joy, I oftentimes sat scrutinizing myself to find out why I had missed all that marital joy during my life's journey and remembered what David had been telling me repeatedly "You want me to do things that you expect me to do." He was so right because I did expect him to fulfill his duty as a husband and the commandment of the Lord as written in Ecclesiastes 9:9 "Enjoy life with your wife, whom you love, all the days of this meaningless life that God has given you under the sun--all the meaning less days. For this is your lot in life and in your toilsome labor under the sun."

But he rebelled against the Lord, and that broke my heart and shattered the dream I had desired to make my house a holy sanctuary of worship and love. Moreover, exactly like all other women who expect love from their husbands, I expected the same from him. When a woman leaves behind her parental home for a man, she leaves behind her family, her luxury, and the love and care she gets from them. All that is a big sacrifice she makes to be with her husband to fulfill her dream of being married happily ever after. But my marriage proved its worth by making me realize that dreams are just meant to be dreams. They are fictional and have no relevance to reality. Being left isolated, I had lost my identity. Like every other female, I also had the inborn instinct to care, sacrifice, serve, and love the one who belonged to me so that I could display those emotions through my acts to complete my identity. I had no one to love or shower my love and had to silence my inner yearnings, like the footprints washed by the passerby on the seashore. Choking within me were my emotions, as I was unable to neither cry nor speak it out loud. Having no child or pet to cuddle with or to love and to be loved. Just living my life on oxygen without fellowship and friendship and breathing only to survive the days allotted to my account. But now all that was history, as I had deleted all my yearnings and no longer desired anything from David, which had set me free of all the expectations and attachments I had from him earlier. Life became good as the peace of the Lord had dawned on me. I sat in the calm of my settled emotions, thanking God each day in my prayers. The pious and serene atmosphere of my home and the surrounding view of the beach emulated His glory, which seemed to be a perfect place for me. I relaxed in peace and harmony with the mesmerizing sound of the soft rustling of the tall coconut trees swaying in full swing as the towering tides kept lashing across the seashore. Just to send their positive vibrations around me. Where my eyes feasted daily on the gorgeous view of the golden orb as it peeked out, breaking the dawn to shimmer its bright streaks, announcing each day my time to meet the Lord; then I sat near the open window to worship, while the fresh, cool breeze caressed my face to give me the feel of His touch. Moreover, the fragrance of the jasmine flowers from across the bungalow enhanced my spiritual aura and the sound of the chirping birds created a perfect ambiance for me to savor the Lord's presence. Time kept passing by, and so did months. David often called me up to share that he was enjoying his retirement and was doing good. He also kept forwarding me the pictures of the new renovation that he had done to our home in the U.S. and other pictures of the yard. On one of those days, he shared with me that his son had divorced his wife and had broken his home, which had saddened his heart and had hit him hard. Then I told him, "I probably think he made a wrong choice in life." But within my heart, I knew that God the Father had given David back the return gift to be hurt by his own son, to make him realize how much pain he had caused to his own father. The God of the universe. For it is written in Psalms 119:136, "Rivers of water run down my eyes because men do not keep their law."

CHAPTER 17

DEFYING GOD'S INTERVENTION

I am what I am, I'm not going to change anyway.

It was a Sunday afternoon, August 20, when David called to share his testimony with me and said, "I felt strongly convicted in my Spirit that I need to call you to sort out things that had been frustrating me for a long time. The main reason is that I cannot discern why you have not yet planned to return home." These words saddened my heart, as he had been emotionally hurting and disgracing me time and time again, by crossing all boundaries of humanity, loyalty courtesy and respect to demean and to torment me. So, just to freshen up his mind, I reminded him of the things that he kept saying to me. "I can only provide you here with food and shelter and nothing more. There is nothing here for you to do. You can go and fulfill your dreams in India." He added, "That was our past. The past is gone, but we need to live for today and for this moment. If we keep going back, we can never move forward and make any progress." I then replied, "That is so true." Having realized that I was already choked, David decided not to pursue any further conversation with me and said, "Ok, I will talk to you tomorrow when you feel better. You take care, bye for now." After he hung up, I could not figure out nor decipher what he wanted from me after damaging my trust and destroying everything. Feeling emotionally perturbed and wary, I tried to stop my thought process, knowing that muddy water is best cleared up by leaving it all alone. I tried to focus on the lead that came from the silence of my soul, knowing full well that the Lord would play out the plan that he had already predestined for my life. After a great struggle, I succeeded to get my peace back to go on with my normal routine.

My phone rang again in the evening, at 7 p.m. It was David on WhatsApp. I attended his call, and he calmly said, "This is really serious talk. Don't take it lightly by ignoring it this time, as you have always been doing in the past. So, I am repeating it again; please hear carefully. Ever since we were married, I have thought about the issues that we have had in our marriage. The main problem that I could see was the communication gap, which made it difficult for us to understand each other. And in spite of knowing the fact that we both are godly people and don't think bad about each other nor have any bad intentions. You kept misunderstanding me for everything that I would say to you by misinterpreting it in a negative manner. And despite me explaining to you that you are my wife, whom I would never hurt, you never felt obliged to concede to it. This has been so frustrating for me, as I kept struggling for years to explain to you that it is your own interpretation and not what I had said to you. But you misconstrued my innocent statements, and rather than asking me what I really meant, you earmarked those statements as mean. This saddens me a lot, knowing that even in my wildest dreams, I would not want to do that to my wife. And all this has always been blocking any improvement that I desired to make in our relationship. Then how do you think it is possible for me to move forward when deep down I could not liberate myself from the feeling of guilt? And do you know by doing all that, you kept killing me inside?" Then he said," Can I ask you a couple of questions now?" I replied, "Yes." He continued, "Are you exempt from certain Biblical principles just because you are an emotional person?" Then I said, "No, not at all." Then he said, "What does Biblical forgiveness mean to you, being a woman of God? Is it right in the sight of the Lord to bring up all the past hurts of all the years as if they all happened yesterday? Because that is not forgiveness. I therefore request you to scrutinize yourself, whether you have been walking in the way of the Lord by applying His Word into your life." I replied to him, "I have forgiven you, but I am unable to heal myself, and I tried to remind you of the past things so that you don't repeat them again to hurt me." Then he said, "The Lord is a Mighty God who has forgiven your sins by dying on the cross for you. Then, is it not your duty to forgive me? Read Mathew 6:15 'But if ye forgive not men their trespasses, neither will your Father forgive your trespass.'" Then I said, "Yes, so true, you are right. I agree with you; I need to do that." Then he requested me to deeply meditate on all the things that he had spoken to me and upon all the Bible verses that talk about forgiveness. He bid me goodbye, saying, "I will let go of you, take care, love you." After he hung up, I kept pondering upon his words and felt the need to re-read forgiveness verses. I just wanted to scrutinize myself and find out how I have failed the Lord by walking in my own ways. And all that made me restless, and I was like a fish out of the pond tossing and turning on my bed, praying till I dozed off.

The next morning, when I woke up, all that David had said to me was fresh on my mind. So, after taking my shower, I sat down to have my exclusive prayer time with the Lord and started reading and meditating on the verses. I realized that forgiveness was not about the person who has wronged you but about your own personal peace and spiritual growth. That reminded me of Peter asking the Lord, how oft shall my brother sin against me, and I forgive him? And this was the reply he got from the Lord, as quoted in Matthew 18:22 "Jesus said to him,

"I do not say to you, up to seven times, but up to seventy-seven times." Similarly, the Lord had also forgiven even those who had crucified Him without a cause by saying, "Father, forgive them, for they do not know what they do." Luke 23:34.

Immediately, the Spirit of repentance fell on me, and I started asking the Lord for forgiveness, feeling that David have not known what he was doing to me. And I kept on misjudging him by earmarking his statements as negative, thinking that he says all these things to me because he hates me. So, I wept bitterly before the Lord, asking Him to forgive me for the sin I had committed by blaming an innocent person who did not even know how he was ruining our relationship. I prayed and prayed for long, repenting before the Lord by taking responsibility for the wrong I had done to hurt David. I felt His peace. It was the first time in years that I realized I was wrong in our marital relationship.

David called me the next morning, and I narrated to him how the Bible verse had convicted me to realize that probably you also must not have known how you were hurting me. Exactly like the ones who crucified Lord Jesus. So, I repented before the Lord, asking Him to forgive me for judging your statements to be mean. Then I told David, "I am really sorry, and from now on, I will ask you first what you mean before I misjudge you." David replied, "That is really amazing to know that the Lord has answered my prayer and blessed you with wisdom. I had been asking the Lord to make you understand that you have not been acting towards me according to the Bible's teachings. Trusting that He will someday hear and answer my prayer to change things between us. And knowing that if that change comes, it would be the result of His divine intervention, and now that you have had a revelation from the Lord, I am so happy, and I lift my praise to God - thanking Him. To whom all the power and the glory belong."

But even after David admitted that the revelation I had from the Lord was an answer to his prayer to change things between us, David made the 'divine intervention' of the Lord null and void. To my shock, his whole attitude changed towards me after I took the blame and the responsibility that I had misconstrued his innocent statements. It seemed to me that fear gripped his heart at the mere thought of our reconciliation. Soon, he called to say that he was leaving for the Upper Midwest, probably to get guidance and advice from his relative about his next move. Later, when he called me on WhatsApp, he shared pictures of all the chores he did for his family. I complimented him for the pictures and wrote, "It's an amazing gesture of your love to be involved in family projects. Plus, a lovely chance for you to spend quality time with them. I really do admire that, but don't you think that I am your family with whom you should also spend some time?" Then he immediately got wild and said, "Why are you talking to me like that?" Then I said, "Why can't I say that? I am your wife and your family." He shouted back and said, "It is so close to the truth. I do not want you to discuss our past." After hearing that from him, I realized how he had lost the last chance that the Lord gave him to reconcile. I knew our Lord was a God of patience and, in His mercy, had given David the last chance to mitigate the strife before he settled the score. But Satan had cunningly brainwashed and blinded David to not even register the Divine Intervention of the Lord.

My spiritual warfare started to overcome all by the Word of the Lord and by the power of the Holy Blood as time kept passing by. It was late at night when I received a call from David, and he said, "Can I ask you a question?" I said, "Sure, why not." He asked, "Since you have not yet planned to return home, then why can't I sell our house and rent a house in the Upper Midwest to stay there? My relatives are anxiously waiting for me to move there." I replied, "If your relatives are your family, then is not your wife also your family? Why would you not come here to Mumbai and stay with me for some time, and then we can return to the U.S. and sell our house to move over to the Upper Midwest?" He replied, "Why would I come to India? I don't like it. Moreover, what will I come and do there? I am happy here and plan to put our house on the market and rent an apartment to be close to my lovely family in the Upper Midwest." I asked, "How come you have decided and planned everything by your own consent without even discussing anything with me? Don't you think I have an equal marital rite to say and choose where and what property we need to buy?" He stated, "I have finally decided that I am going to enjoy my life and live the way I want, how I want, and where I want. I am what I am, and I am not going to change anyway." Moreover, I am not the one who is going to sit here and crib about you not coming back home. You will be happy staying there in India, and I am happy staying here all by myself. There is no solution to all this." I responded, "If you have already made a final decision to stay separately without me, then why should we be connected? If you think there is no solution to this, then I can give you a fantastic suggestion that you really deserve. Divorce is my final solution for you. Period." His last remark was, "I am not going to discuss anything with you further. I will let you go." He then hung up.

CHAPTER 18

DAILY DOSES OF NARC'S NONSENSE

Time stood still, and nothing changed between us. I got busy healing my wounds, just like the desperate gushing waves trying to wash the stale footsteps on the wet, muddy sand. David, on the other hand, kept calling me to give me all the good news he had, stating that he was doing well and managing well by preparing his own meals. He kept sending me pics for months of renovation that he was doing at his relative's house by paying several visits to the Upper Midwest. He said that he felt extremely ecstatic and blessed to be close to his family. The Bible says, "Therefore shall a man leave his father and mother, and shall cleave to his wife; and they shall be one flesh." Genesis 2:24

These messages proved what a rebellious man of God he was, defying God's purpose for marriage. The messages that he kept sending me made things easy for me as he shared his outsourced fake joy. His traits proved that he was an insecure, lonely, neglected kid who was deprived of real love since childhood, which had completely damaged him. All that made me feel very, very sorry for him. Knowing that he was chronologically unhappy and had desired to be happy, he had his mind set on seeking validation from external sources from his so-called family. He foolishly forgot how he had sabotaged his own personal relationship with God through his transgression. In God's kingdom, every season is a temporary season. The first season makes you sow in pain, but the next season comes with joy to reap the fruits of its prosperity. It's exactly like the rough, rejected gold thrown down first, to be burned into a furnace, to later make it come out shining bright and glittering for tomorrow. Likewise, my pain chastened me to come out strong to face the forthcoming days of my bright future. The Lord God had destined that I waste no more of my precious time by involving myself in David's stupid cat-mouse race, which gave him the highs to torture me. The Bible verse says in Hebrews 4:12-13 "Nothing in all creation is hidden from God. Everything is uncovered and laid bare before the eyes of him we must give account."

God knew all the secrets of his heart. He was well aware of David's transgressions, swing moods, and instability that he manipulated to dip me down into a deep pit. But unfortunately, he failed miserably, as I had already dropped him like a hot potato by walking out of his life. One day, he would say, "You are my wife. Period."

The next day, then... I am no longer visible to him in his own house. Then, another time, he would say, "I love you in my own way," and then next time, he would say, "But, how can I love you when I was not in love with you before marriage?" What a silly, sick, stupid, immature statement of his. Then, one fine morning, he agreed that we should get divorced. Then, after months of struggle to make me get rid of all my stuff, by distributing and emptying all my cupboards with my ticket in hand to leave for India, he took a wild U-turn and said, "The Lord God spoke to me, and said, I would be at fault if I divorced you now, after being happy and getting along so well with you. Now, I don't want to divorce you." Then, being bugged, I told him, "What you have started, I will finish. Now, I will divorce you." He then secretly withdrew the divorce case by calling the lawyer that he had hired. Then he planned a lavish trip to enjoy a Roman holiday with me. Then, after the holiday, his unstable swing mood took a double U-turn, and he said, "We have nothing in common." That was such a foolish, hilarious statement to hear from him again. Surely, I did not understand what he wanted me to have in common with him. The only thought that occurred to my mind was it could not be caste or creed. But it could be our organs that are different, which probably he could have forgotten to register that I was a female and not a male. All this sounded to me like a real comedy story of an immature, underdeveloped kid, which made my friends giggle a lot when I narrated to them these daily doses of his nonsensical statements during my farewell party before leaving for America for my court case. But that was still more of a HA HA HA for my friends and a hot topic of fun. When I shared with them that David had now paid, and approached my law company to serve him a notice of divorce. Then my friends giggled and giggled and said, "He withdrew his first divorce due to fear of God, and now he has paid for the divorce." HA HA HA. Then my other friend said, "Super bumper U-turn." Did God tell him, "I am sorry, I have changed my mind? You pay the penalty immediately and get divorced right now without further delay." Oh my God, that was so hilarious; we all giggled and laughed our guts out. Then, to add more spice to their joke, I replied, "It's now more and more of ha ha ha's for you. Enjoy." The title of this comedy story is… "Married Once and Divorced Twice." It was a great farewell party of fun to be remembered forever in my book. Forever……

I also shared with them about my revelation that I knew God would transform it into reality. Below is the same message that my friends read on my WhatsApp before my divorce. The message to David on WhatsApp on December 31 stated, "This is my prayer to the Lord for the coming year, and also the promise I have in God. So, I thank God in anticipation of the goodness He holds for my bright future in the coming new year. May you be blessed to do the same prayer for the year." David replied,

"Thanks for the inspiring New Year message. May your year be blessed in every way and every situation you encounter on the way."

My next message to David on January 1 of the new year said, "My Dearest Hubby, I pray that you be blessed with all that you have longed for, consistently worked for, and religiously pursued, may be achieved by you in this coming New Year. And all that is not meant for you, from God, I pray, may the Lord God eliminate that person away from your life."

Then, I forwarded him a message that I liked. During the class at Fresno Pacific University, the speaker asked one of the spouses in the audience: "Does your husband make you happy?" The husband stood up straight, showing much confidence at that moment, knowing his wife would say yes because she had never complained about anything during their marriage. However, the wife answered the question with a resounding "No." "No, my husband does not make me happy." The husband was baffled, but the wife continued: "My husband never made me happy, and he does not make me happy. Whether I am happy or not is not dependent on him but on me. I am the only person on whom happiness depends. I choose to be happy in every situation, and every moment of my life, for if my happiness depended on another person, thing, or circumstance, I would be in serious trouble. I need to decide to be happy regardless of anything that happens.

Whether I own a lot or little. I am happy! Whether I'm going out with my husband or staying home alone. I am married, but I was already happy when I was single. I'm happy for myself. I love my life not because my life is easier than anyone else's but because I have decided to be happy as an individual. I am responsible for my own happiness. I have taken this obligation from my husband and everyone else. I free them from the burden of carrying them on their mother's shoulders. It makes everyone's life lighter. Never give anyone the responsibility to control your happiness. Be happy. If it's hot, if you are sick, if you have no money, even if anyone has hurt you, not valued you, nor loved you. Be happy and love yourself."

I had the same philosophy and had endured living my married life to my own abilities. I was happy with myself, mainly for two reasons. First and foremost, being lonely and alone in my bedroom was a blessing in disguise that made me develop a deeper relationship with the Lord. Secondly, I was grateful for the thrill of the joy of the Lord, who surprised me each day by knitting my family drama story and prompting me to write that I may have the privilege to share His testimonies across the nations to glorify Him. Days passed by, and the right time arrived for me to catch my flight from the Chhatrapati Shivaji International Airport in Mumbai to reach Chicago O'Hare International Airport. I waited to board the flight. I prayed and opened my Bible randomly, and as I read the verse, I held myself in peace, having the assurance from the Lord that now I shall see the Egyptian of my life no more forever. Exodus 14:13 says, “Fear ye not, stand still, and see the salvation of the Lord, which he will shew you today: for the Egyptians whom you have seen today, ye shall see them again no more forever. The Lord shall fight for you, and ye shall hold your peace.” With this beautiful verse of promise on my lips, I boarded the flight to reach Chicago O’Hare International Airport.

CHAPTER 19

FROM CAPTIVITY TO FREEDOM

The D-Day arrived. I landed at Chicago O'Hare International Airport. David came to fetch me there, and then we drove back to Wisconsin. When I entered my house, I was taken aback seeing all the renovation David had done outwardly and inside the house. All the furniture settings in my house were changed. My drawing room sofa set was shifted aside, and my TV was set opposite the huge dual recliners. My dining table was full of all sorts of medicines, papers, and other items. My chandelier that hung below over my rose vase was pulled upwards, my roses in the vase were rearranged, and the tap fittings in the kitchen were new. David, having noticed my expression of shock, said that he had shifted all this to place my bed in the TV room downstairs so that I could be more comfortable there. Then he brought in my luggage and left to retire upstairs. I was extremely tired and exhausted after this long journey from Mumbai to London, then from

London to Chicago, and from Chicago to Wisconsin. I wanted to freshen up, so when I entered my washroom area and opened the cabinet, I found none of my bathing stuff there but noticed half-used body wash, creams, oils, accessories, etc. It was very disgusting to know that someone had the audacity to first enter my house in my absence, then use my personal toilet, and on top of it, remove my items and replace them with her own stuff! I believe that even if it had been David's friend who would have seen this happening to her, she would have surely thrown out all the stuff outside the house. Forget, then, what a wife would do. But on the contrary, I thought I was blessed that the Lord had shown me David's true colors. The Bible says, "And you shall know the truth, and the truth shall free you." John 8:32.

But I was already free and cared a damn about David and his secret activities. I then had a nice hot shower and then dozed out to bed. The next morning, when I woke up, David was not at home and had already left for his office. Then I did my prayers and had my breakfast, and later, after emptying my suitcase, I organized all my clothes to keep them in my cupboard. Later, I decided to prepare meals. When I opened my kitchen cabinet, I was amazed to see different kinds of nonveg food packets, a typical variety of spices, salsas, hot red chili sauces, etc., which David had never eaten ever since the day I had married him. Later in the evening, when David arrived, we sat down to watch the news and have dinner. Then I asked, "Since when have you created the taste of hot spicy food? He replied, "I have my life to live." Then, after supper, we both watched a movie and retired to our bedrooms. Soon, things changed between us, and David stopped having supper at home and was usually out late in the evening. Sometimes, he would go early in the evenings, well dressed, which prompted me to think that he was out on a date. He would then say bye in a rush and walk out, and I would say, "Enjoy! and have a great evening ahead." The Bible verse says, "There is a way that seems right to a man, but its end is the way to death." Proverbs 14:12.

Most of the day, I spent writing my lovely, lonely love story, and in the evenings, my friend Julie would come over to edit my book. Time kept passing by, and I was anxiously awaiting to hear from my lawyer's end about his meeting with David's lawyer. David informed me that he had hired the most experienced and efficient Law Company in Wisconsin, which knew all about the Indian and Wisconsin divorce laws.

But he had hired the same lawyer who had submitted my divorce papers earlier, which David withdrew later, stating that it was the Lord who had convicted him not to go ahead with the divorce proceedings. More than a month had passed, and neither of our lawyers had finalized any terms of negotiations for both of us. We were impatiently waiting to hear from their end. The divorce date was approaching, and David informed me that if we missed this date, the next date would come after six months. I told David I would neither wait here for a second, even after my divorce nor will I ever come back to America again. I will see that I sort out this issue before I leave for India permanently. David replied, "It is not so easy to deal with these prestigious Law companies. They know their job pretty well." I sensed that he probably was insisting, knowing that his company would definitely draft out all the terms in his favor. Then I told him, "Even if they draft in your favor and we don't agree among ourselves, the divorce will anyhow get delayed." I insisted that we should sit together and settle amongst ourselves. It's our divorce, and we don't need to depend on lawyers by giving our reins into their hands. He then brought the pad, and I noted down all the details of our property and amicably settled amongst ourselves. Then, I asked David to print out the final draft, and we both signed it. The next morning, I called my lawyer, and his secretary said that he was not in the office but in court. I then literally begged her to get me some time from him, and she said he usually returns back from the court at 5 p.m. Then I asked her if I could come today, and she said, "I am not sure, but you can still take a chance."

Later, when Julie arrived, we both immediately drove off to the lawyer's office in Wisconsin Rapids. Luckily, we reached there ahead of time. Later, when my lawyer entered the office, he saw me and smiled. Then I told him, "I have come to see you." He nodded and said, "Okay." Then he called me in, and we both entered his room. Then, I tried to explain to him that I needed his favor. I told him that my return air ticket to India was booked, my seats were reserved and confirmed, and there was no way that I could change or extend my departure date now. "I will have to leave for India immediately," I said, "and I request you to continue with the proceedings so that I can be done with David forever."

My lawyer said, "I have been extremely busy, and I have not yet had any meeting with David's lawyer to finalize the negotiations between you two." Then I took out the draft from my purse and handed it over to him. He read it and said, "How can David settle for this and that, and how could you agree for so and so?" I then replied, "I have no other option except to agree with him." He was satisfied, and then we both left his office, thanking him.

Then, the next day, early morning, David got a call from his lawyer, who asked him to report to her office. David then left. I later called Julie and asked her to accompany me to the court case tomorrow. She said she would surely do that for me.

I was then at peace, and I remembered the Bible verse of the Lord's promise "For I am the Lord your God who takes hold of your right hand and says to you, do not fear

I will help you." Isaiah 41:13. Then I prayed, thanking the Lord God Almighty, and retired to bed.

The next morning, when I woke up, I got a call from a newspaper company that my testimony had been published in *The Wisconsin Christian Newspaper.* The concerned person said it was a full-page coverage that was ready to be released today. He also said I was welcome to come and collect my first copy. I then thanked him, and I was extremely happy thanking my loving God, whose mercies are new each day. For what a joyful thing He had made to happen to release it on this day of all the other days!

Then, when Julie came to fetch me, we first went and picked up the copy from the newspaper office and then drove straight to the court. David was not to be seen anywhere, nor were either of our lawyers. The judge had also not arrived, and we both went and sat down in the courtroom. There were a few more people already seated there. The judge then arrived, and so did David and our lawyers. Then, David's name was called out, and he went ahead and took the oath. The judge then cross-questioned him, and later, my name was called out. I also left and took the oath. The judge then asked me a few questions, "Are you sure you need this divorce?" I replied, "I am not so foolish to repeat this same mistake of compromising again for the second time. I am sure and positive that I need this divorce right now." Then, all the people in the courtroom laughed. The order was then passed that we were divorced, and I was granted to use my maiden name.

When we got out of the courtroom, I was like an unflappable personality- calm and serene without a pinch of pain. I walked up to David, shook hands, congratulated him, and asked him if I could take him out for lunch to celebrate the divorce ceremony. He said, "This is sad," and I laughed and said, "Why sad? You should be happy that the Lord has answered your prayer." He felt humiliated, and suddenly, his face changed color, and he was unable to face me. He said, "You both carry on," and he quickly walked out. Then Julie and I went to a lovely restaurant, had wine, said cheers, and celebrated the Lord's plan, remembering Titus 3:10-11 "Reject a divisive man after the first and the second admonition; knowing that such a person is warped and sinning being self-condemned." We then laughed, joked, had lunch, read the newspaper write-up, and had a lot of fun together.

CHAPTER 20

DETACHMENT - BOON IN DISGUISE

The detachment was a boon in disguise for me. It was now my time to live my life without responsibilities, without liabilities, and to live without hearing any more of David's vicious, venomous outpouring of comments.

The Bible verse says, "A good man out of the good treasure of his heart brings forth good, and an evil man out of the evil treasure of his heart brings forth evil. For out of the abundance of the heart, his mouth speaks." Luke 6:14

I was eager and desperate to leave this house immediately and shift somewhere else, but the main problem was that it was impossible for me to find temporary accommodation for just a few weeks. Then, after much searching, I decided to compromise against my desires and concentrated on accomplishing my job. I then started sorting out all my stuff by making separate piles of each of the different items that I had. My whole living room, my porch room, and my bedroom were then full of all my stuff. My friends' calls started coming, asking me for the time of their visit to my house to pick up things that they needed. Some paid for my exclusive outfits and bought them, while others picked them up for free. The good news was that at the right time, I got a call from the manager of the organization that my booth had been booked at the Yearly Cultural Exhibition to be held in Wisconsin. I was glad that my Lord brought this opportunity for me at the perfect time to ease my burden. The Bible verse says, "Come to me all you who labor and are heavy laden, and I will give you rest. For My yoke is easy, and My burden is light." Matthew 11:28-30

Meanwhile, David kept himself busy with his office and his usual activities, and after one week, he said that he was leaving for the Upper Midwest to look for his new house. I kept searching for charity trusts where I could donate my remaining things. I was really exhausted, for it was not easy for me to shift to a different country and handle all this by myself. Moreover, before leaving for his trip, David said, "I am no longer responsible for you. You need to hire some income tax company to take charge of your taxes and a chartered accountant to file your own taxes here in the USA." I knew not the A B C's of taxes, as David had been filing joint income taxes ever since we had been married. But I just knew one thing, I knew Jesus very well.

The Bible verse says, "I will instruct you and teach you in the way you should go; I will guide you with My eye." Psalm 32:8.

It exactly happened the same the next morning; the spirit nudged me to go to the Head Office to learn more about the withdrawal formalities of the Fidelity Investments Funds. It was about my share that we both had split and had settled. Then, when I met the lady concerned who managed the Fidelity Funds, she explained to me all about its pros and cons, took my signatures, and handed me all the documents. Then I told the lady I knew that I would be taxed heavily for the total withdrawal of my funds. But I know not a single Tax Consulting Company who can file my taxes for... then before I could complete my whole sentence, she was interrupted by an incoming call, and spoke to someone, and then told that gentleman, "I have a lady seated before me, who needs to file the taxes for her Fidelity amount that she has just received after her Divorce, and asked him if he would do the needful for me, the gentleman then replied "Sure," to her.

Then, immediately, she handed me over all the documents that she had drafted. I thanked her for her kind help and left in a jiffy to the Lawyer's office, as it was time for his office to be closed.

I reached there minutes before 5 p.m. The gentleman was very kind and polite. I then handed him over all the documents, asked him for his fees, filled out his forms, completed all the necessary formalities, and hired him to do what was needed. I then thanked my Lord for instructing, guiding, and leading me to the right helpful person. Then, when David arrived back from his trip, I paid him the rent of $200 for the month of June for staying in my own house. The next day, it was Sunday, and we both went to church together. Most of the church members were quite amazed to see both of us together after the divorce. Many asked me questions about how I could still be with him after the divorce. I replied, "I am good enough that God gave me this ability to make the right decisions, like Jesus, of how to treat those who hurt you the most." Time passed, and later, David started going to church at 7 a.m., prior to the usual church service time at 10 a.m.

My friend, Pastor Buki, then invited me to attend her church, and every Sunday, she requested her assistant to go and fetch me and drop me back. It was a lot of fun with all of the activities in her church. We all had meals together after the service, and everybody brought in a new dish each Sunday morning. Soon, I started going out with my church friends to shop for things for my family and friends, as well as things for myself that weren't available in India. I visited banks to close all my ministry accounts and to check my personal account, which David had separated from our joint account. I started distributing gifts to all my friends and kept sending gifts to pastors' wives in different cities in America. I invited church ladies to come and pick all the stuff that each liked. Then, I arranged to ship my two suitcases in advance to rid myself of the burden. The shipping company guy said, "Ma'am, for security and safety reasons, we only collect those suitcases that are wrapped in cardboard boxes. They don't get scratched, nor can anyone steal the stuff out of them. Then Julie came to my rescue, and we both went hunting for the box at all the different malls, asking them if they had any boxes for sale or in their storehouses, but we failed. My flight date was approaching, and I just waited on the Lord. The shipment guy kept on calling me, as the shipment of his other customers was all ready to be shipped to India. I then requested him to give me some more time.

Early the next morning, Julie called me and said, "You will not believe this! Yesterday evening, my new refrigerator arrived prior to its delivery date, packed in a huge cardboard box. I was excited; I opened it carefully so that the box would not be torn, and I also saved the wrapped strips for you." It was amazing when she brought it to my house, to see that it was exactly the same size as my huge suitcase. David then helped me, and we both started pasting the address labels on all the sides of the boxes. Then, in the early morning, the guy arrived, checked the boxes, and took the delivery.

I was very pleased that I had emptied all my cupboards, leaving behind not even a needle in this house.

The Bible verse says, "And he led them forth by the right way, that they might go to a city for a dwelling place." Psalm 107:7

Thus, according to this promise, I was all ready for my new dwelling place, quickening to finish all my remaining formalities. I paid my rent, which was due to David, for all the extra months of staying in my house. I attended all the farewell parties that my different friends arranged for me. Finally, the day arrived, and I left with David for the Chicago O'Hare International Airport. Then David dropped me at the main entrance door and left to park his car. Then I proceeded further towards the baggage scanner, got my bags scanned, collected my boarding pass, and walked out when David arrived. We both then sat down on the bench like two strangers. I asked David to supervise my luggage and went to the restroom to freshen up myself. I then asked David if he could leave now, but he waited for some time till I walked in for my immigration checkup and then left. I got the best seat, and soon, the flight took off, and my jumbled, mingled mind was at peace. Later, the beverages were served, and I had a glass of wine, then supper, and rested. Finally, the Lord's rest was my portion when I reached safely at my home in Mumbai.

CHAPTER 21

REWRITING MY OWN DESTINY

When I reached Mumbai, I was no more like a broken woman, lacking the confidence to cope with my life. To restart my life, I had already deleted all the Satanic distractions of negative vibes in my life. I was on a clean slate, ready to rewrite my own destiny. It was through God's mercy that I already had a beautiful apartment in Bandra West, Mumbai, the best locality known as the "Queen of the Suburbs," to permanently settle thereafter. I had two servants to serve me with God's blessings. Thus, I was relieved from the burden of cooking. For it was His good pleasure and will that I invest all the time in Him.

The Bible verse says, "For it is God who works in you both to will and to do for his good pleasure." Philippians 2:13

But before I could fulfill God's will, I was thrust with many personal things to settle myself. My first priority was to have a good rest after the jetlag, and secondarily, to open all my suitcases and put all my stuff in order.

The wardrobes that I had in Mumbai were already jam-packed with my clothes. There was no way I could fit four suitcases worth of stuff in it, so I had to arrange for a contractor who would bring his team in to paint my entire house and make two new wardrobes for me. It was a very long struggle to find one, as it was the season of Diwali, a Hindu New Year when most of the contractors were extremely tied up with other big assignments. Finally, I got a contractor who signed a contract with me, promising that he would complete my job as soon as possible, but instead, he completed it after months of delay.

During that struggle, my health kept deteriorating, as it was too much for me to handle and supervise all the painters and carpenters who kept working in my house till late hours. I was tired and exhausted, and later, one night, I started shivering in my bed, so I casually covered myself with a couple of blankets and dozed out. The next day, my head started burning, and when I checked my temperature, I had a high fever. I then called Dr. Raju Shah at the Belfer Clinic, who sent his nurse to my place to take my blood sample. When the reports came, it was confirmed that I had Dengue fever, and my platelet count was very low. The doctor then advised that I should be admitted to the hospital immediately without further delay. I packed my accessories, etc., and left for the hospital. It was a very long process to go through different departments to comply with the admission formalities by signing and filling out different forms. I had no strength to even stand. But it was God's mercy that when I reached the booking window, I was lucky to get the best available single private room for my stay. The treatment then started immediately, and the doctors kept visiting me according to their shifts. All of my tests were repeated again according to different doctor's opinions, and I was kept on a drip that the nurses kept monitoring. I had nothing else to do there except to lie on the bed and to call upon the Lord's name. The Bible verse says, "Now I know that the Lord saves His anointed; He will answer them from His holy heaven with the saving strength of His right hand."

Psalm 20:6

I knew nothing was impossible in His kingdom, and gradually, I started recouping by calling upon His name. My prayers were answered, my recovery quickened, and He recouped me completely to return back safely home. His Word says, "No weapon that is formed against thee shall prosper." Isaiah 54:17

Then, after my recovery, my A.B. Insurance Company's representative requested me to submit all the bills and reports to him so that he could file for my refund from the A.B. Insurance Company for the amounts that I had paid in advance to the Hinduja Hospital in Khar

West. Time passed by, and after months, I received an email from A.B. Insurance Company stating, "We have resolved your claim." But what they had resolved they never mentioned... as they were well aware that my policy would expire within a few months and were purposely taking their sweet quality time.

Finally, I received a letter from them stating, "The claim has been declined." I called the A.B. Insurance Company to inquire about their reason for the rejection of the claim. I received another email from them, explaining that I had lied to the company and had hidden the fact that I was suffering from cholesterol and osteoporosis. The email tussle was prolonged for weeks between the insurance company and me. Finally, I got wild and called them, stating that I had bought the policy to be treated for all my ailments, "And do you think I am foolish to pay you huge amounts just to deprive myself of the treatment so that I suffer and get sick?" I bought the policy to safeguard myself and to be treated. Moreover, what do cholesterol and osteoporosis have to do with Dengue fever in order to delay my claim? The tussle continued, and after weeks, I got a call from one of the lady employees of the A.B. Insurance Company. I gave her a bit of my mind. I told her, "Go and inform your company that you have defamed me by calling me a liar, stating that I had hidden facts from you. I am a woman of God, and I don't speak lies. I will sue the company big-time by claiming huge amounts. I don't care about the petty bills that I have paid; they're just peanuts for me. I am a servant of God, and I look for justice and my rightful dues. Even if you pay this amount, I will give it to charity for the poor and will send you proof of that. I have the ministry to serve God, known as the 'LOVE4-ALL.' I serve society and the true living God. I walk in His statutes, and lies are not my cup of tea. It's for those who have not yet known the true God Jesus. It's your company that is lying."

I was much too disturbed at that moment and told her, "Before buying my policy, I got all my tests done and submitted the copy to your Insurance Company to verify my health status for their approval. The company first scrutinized my reports and then confirmed that they would would issue the policy to me. They demanded that I pay them an extra Rs 11000 as my coverage for osteoporosis, but the coverage amount to cover my cholesterol, they did not ask for, since my reports showed that I had no cholesterol issues. The lady was dumb and had nothing else to say to me. I then said "bye" to her and disconnected the call.

I lodged the complaint with the government company known as "Insurance Ombudsman" and forwarded them the copy of the denied claim, plus a copy of it to my A.B. Insurance Company. My insurance company was probably shaken, having known the action I had taken, and immediately, within two days, they refunded me Rs

211285/- my full policy amount by depositing the check into my bank account and closing my policy.

But no matter what all happened to me in the outer trials of this tussle, inwardly, I was completely at ease and in peace. I had full faith in my God, and I was sure the victory would be mine. For truth always prevails, but lie fails.

I informed Ombudsmen Insurance that A.B. Insurance had closed my policy and credited Rs 211285, my full amount, back to my bank. The message I got from them was, "Declining claim on a false pretext and cancellation of the policy is a highly irregular and illegal decision." I knew it was the Lord who had fought this battle for me and had allowed the insurance company to be caught in its own trap by making them take this illegal, boorish move.

Later, after weeks of delay, I got a call at 8 p.m. on Saturday from the top doctor from A.B. Insurance Company, informing me that our court case was on Sunday (tomorrow) morning. I was surprised, as I had received no intimation or email from the Ombudsman Insurance Company. The doctor then explained certain things and requested me to withdraw the complaint against the A.B. Insurance Company and said, "Our company has agreed to continue your policy as usual and will be reimbursing your full claim amount soon." I replied, "It sounds good."

The doctor then asked me if I could draft a letter for her so that she could immediately forward it to the Ombudsman Insurance Company to stop the hearing before the next morning. I then wrote the letter stating, "We, both parties, have mutually compromised and request you to kindly dismiss our case before any further hearing." I forwarded it to her. The doctor was very pleased and said, "We are sorry for the trouble we have put you through due to some misinterpretation of your reports." She thanked me for being kind and considerate and for settling the claim amicably. The company was thus put to shame by the Lord's will, and I later received a letter of the award from the A. B. Insurance Company.

I then changed my previous relationship manager, who had played a dirty game by manipulating my health records for his own benefit, over to a new person. I hired Mr. Apurva, a God-fearing guy who owns an insurance company, to deal with my A.B. Insurance Company. He then got me the entire claim refund, plus Rs 40000 extra from the A.B. Insurance Company. Fighting with a huge established company and suing them was no joke. It was the Lord who intervened on my behalf to add another testimony to my life to display His grandeur and glory.

Covid-19 was soon in full swing. It was difficult to go out to do any chores during the quarantine. My contractors and workers left for their villages to seek their own safety, and one of my maids was taken ill. Satan attacked me again, and I started bleeding. That tortured me a lot. The homeopathy pills gave me no relief, and the bleeding increased. Finally, I decided to get the surgery done, and I started my Google search to look for the best doctors available in Mumbai. Luckily, a Clin Tech India video ad appeared before me, explaining a new technology. It was about the new surgical laser treatment center in Mumbai that treats anorectal issues. I watched the video and immediately dialed the number and got the secretary online of a well-known doctor. The secretary informed me that the doctor was tied up with other prior surgeries and was leaving to go abroad in two days to perform surgeries there. Henceforth, he will not be able to do my surgery. But after my request, I was blessed to get my appointment scheduled that very evening by his secretary to meet the doctor. I was extremely happy, and I reached the clinic in time and was asked to fill in the forms first. The doctor called me in. He checked me and my reports and said, "'It's a five-minute job for me to do your surgery, but a lifetime of relief for you." He was kind and said, "Ma'am, you don't have to worry about your insurance or anything. I have tie-ups with all Insurance companies in Mumbai, and we can take care of your insurance coverage only if you have any policy." I thanked him and asked him about my pre-tests. He said, "Regarding your pre-tests, you don't have to worry; I will ask my assistant to arrange for someone to get it done. My secretary will call and inform you before he sends someone to collect your samples. I just want you to chill out and relax for the day I have scheduled your surgery. All you need is to report on Wednesday the 14th at the Apollo Hospital after 12 p.m. I was extremely happy and thanked him for his kind favor.

The surgery was performed, and then I was shifted to rest in my private room to wait for my discharge confirmation. Later, my doctor visited me, put me on a medication dosage schedule, and warned me to relax for a month. Soon, the blisters popped up, and I had excruciating pain. I could hardly sit. But by petitioning and praying to the Lord each day and night, I recouped and recovered soon. For there may be pain in the night, but joy comes in the morning. Thus, my Lord took away all my future sufferings and blessed me to enjoy all different kinds of cuisines, delicious Indian food, and savory, spicy snacks, etc., to munch. The insurance company approved the payment for the final bill, and through God's timely intervention, my money was saved and the surgery was done free of cost.

My next priority was to acquire all of my ID documents to comply with the rules and regulations of the Government of India. Moving to another country was not easy for me, but it was a hassle. I had to restart everything from scratch since David had closed our joint bank account in America. I did not have an NRE (Non-Residential External) bank account in India, and it was necessary for me to open one here, especially after having obtained citizenship in America. But that was not easy either since I had no specific documents or identity proof to comply with the rules and regulations of the Government of India. I had none of these cards, such as a Voting card or an Aadhaar card. I tried to call different agents to find out the procedures for obtaining these cards. Finally, after complying with all the documentation and demands of the Government agency, I succeeded in applying for the voting card, which was later dispatched to my residence after months. My problems never stopped. Soon, the phone that I had earlier in America stopped working, and I was unable to get the sim card for it in India. I then decided to buy a new phone, but that was not easy either. The phone company wanted my credentials and asked for my Aadhaar card. I had no Aadhaar card. I visited a couple of banks, but I could find none that would issue me the same. Then, my friend informed me that the post office had been authorized to issue Aadhaar cards. The next morning, I left for the post office, where a form was given to me to be filled out. I was called in for my Iris checkup, and later, the guy used a biometric device to capture my fingerprints. He tried thrice and failed and then said, "Ma'am, I am sorry. We can't issue you the Aadhaar card till we get your prints." Then I asked him, "What is the best time to come again?" He replied, "You can come here at 3 p.m." I thanked him, walked out, and perceived a long queue of people waiting outside the post office for their turn to go in. I reached the post office at 3 p.m. sharp, and the guy said, "Ma'am, you are very punctual. Look," pointing at his watch. "It's 3 p.m. sharp." He then took my iris test, and as he was ready to take my fingerprints, I said to him, "Now you will see how punctual my Lord Jesus is." Then I pressed my fingers on the device, trusting the Lord to show His miracle. The guy was quiet, and within seconds, he got crystal clear fingerprints from both my hands and, being amazed, handed me the receipt. Then he questioned me, "What is this about the Lord Jesus' miracle?" I was excited about having an open door, and I then gave him the gospel, and he accepted the Lord. I then prayed for God's wisdom, knowledge, and blessings to come upon him to receive peace, prosperity, and promotion. He then tried to touch my feet. I shrugged and then walked back, explaining to him to be grateful and thankful to the Lord Jesus by touching His feet, Who only is worthy of all glory, praise, and honor.

In the midst of sorting out all these issues of ID cards, problems, and confusion, I was unable to fulfill God's purpose for my life, for which the Lord had clearly instructed me, saying, "When you go to India, go and serve the needy and the poor." But I, myself, had already been very poor in health and had no idea how to serve the needy and the poor. I kept praying and seeking the Lord, trusting that one day, he would open the doors of my ministry. He soon answered my prayer, and after a few months, I saw a pamphlet on my doorstep. It was an invitation from "The Rotary Club of Bandra Bombay" stating that there was an opportunity for those Samaritans who have the desire to serve their community are more than welcome to join the membership of Club. I was glad that the Otters Club venue was very close to my place. I called the number, and Mr. Syedji picked up the phone. I told him, "I would like to join your Rotary Club." He then informed me that it was one of the most prestigious clubs, and the committee decides to enroll members after their status and qualifications are verified and approved. The charges for the yearly membership are Rs 45000. I then agreed to pay that amount, and the next day, he came to fetch me. I had taken my *YOU MAGAZINE* along with me, that had my credentials in it. When we reached the Otters Club venue, I was introduced to all the Rotary members, but no one interviewed me. Mr. Syedji had already handed over my magazine to the President of the Rotary Club to read the coverage. During the meeting time, the President shared my write-up with all of the other members. The lovely buffet was then set up, and I fellowshipped with everyone. My oath ceremony was later scheduled at the Hotel Executive Enclave, where a grand party was held with all the other dignitaries and invitees from different districts of Rotary Clubs. The meeting lasted for a long time as the appreciation of all the members who were involved in big projects and those who had secured huge donations and aid from foreign countries were being mentioned and honored. Later, the banquet was laid to enjoy and celebrate the occasion. I was very happy and soon started attending meetings and getting involved in different projects. The projects were huge, like building wells and homes in remote villages, caring for destitute elderly citizens, distributing food to police personnel, visiting hospitals, arranging blood donation camps, and manufacturing prosthetic legs for the handicapped and young children suffering from cancer, etc. I was grateful to God for giving me this privilege to serve as a Rotarian. The Bible verse says, "Then the righteous will answer Him saying, Lord, when did we see you hungry and feed you, or thirsty and gave you drink? And the King will answer and say to them, 'Assuredly, I say to you, inasmuch you did it to one of the least of these My brethren, you did it to Me.'" Matthew 25:40.

CHAPTER 22

SEEKING GOD – DANIEL FAST

Having so many hectic projects and personal problems, the spirit within me nudged me that I should slow down a bit, leaving aside all into the hands of the Lord. I needed some intimate quality time to be with the Lord, so I started my Daniel fast for twenty-one days, praying for the peace treaty during this world's war crisis to cease, for our church property, for the safety of my family and friends, and for all my funds that have been devoured by petitioning and seeking God to release them. And all of a sudden, the streak of blessing fell upon me. Out of the blue, I received a letter from the Department of the Treasury, Internal Revenue Service from Austin, Texas, regarding The Economic Impact Recovery Rebate during Covid, that read, "Call us to request your refund check." I was excited and started praising and thanking God for His goodness and faithfulness. The next day, late evening, I called the number, praying to get some representative online, and through God's favor, I got a lady representative on the line in a few seconds. She asked me a couple of questions to verify my identity and then said, "Your records confirm that you have not cashed the check that we sent to you for $1800." I replied, "I never received any check." She reconfirmed my Mumbai address, which was correct, and said, "The check should have reached you." I told her, "I'm sorry to state that I did not receive any check even after filling out my tax returns in the Year 2021, but still my amount has been pending since then." She said, "Don't worry. I am going to post your check right now at your Mumbai residence, and I am sure it will reach you." I asked her if she could transfer the funds to my bank directly so that it would be safe for me. She said, "We are not entitled to send checks to any foreign banks besides America." For the second request check, she suggested that I need to fill out a separate form for the next pending installment and then post it to the Philadelphia address either by mail or fax. I tried to fax them from Mumbai and learned that many companies in Mumbai have free fax services to mail letters to America. And found out that none were encrypted but rather scam companies. I didn't want to post it either because it takes months to reach the U.S. I called my best friend Julie in the U.S. and requested her to do what was needed for me. She then took care of it for me. The check then arrived at my residence through the Lord's intervention and by His mercy.

But that was not enough for God, who loved me. He, Who is a cheerful giver, wanted to bless me much more, knowing pretty well about my monetary losses. The story begins when I was in America. I was writing my story on David's laptop since he had locked the computer on which he was busy at home. But when I was finally leaving America, David insisted that I should buy a Mac Pro. My suitcases were all packed, and I was in no mood to add more liabilities to tag this heavy gadget all the way to India. I told him my laptop was sufficient enough for me to handle. But after much persuasion, I bought it. Then, after a long period of time, when I tried to work on it in India, I could not even charge its battery, and after trying it out umpteen times, I was highly frustrated. I took it to the Maple Store, where the team of experts checked it. They gave me the report that there was a problem with the keyboard and suggested that we replace it. I asked them about the cost, and they quoted Rs 40000. I was shocked to hear that, for it was a huge amount. I had no other option left, so I paid for the full amount in advance and then left their store.

But God never left me nor forgot my loss. On January 6 of that year, I received an email from the MacBook Keyboard Litigation Settlement Administrator. The subject was, "If you bought a MacBook laptop sold between 2015 and 2019 equipped with a "Butterfly" Keyboard, you may be eligible for payment from a class action settlement. Please save these numbers to file a claim. It also mentioned that the "Group 1 Settlement Class Members are estimated to receive a payment between $300 and $395." I was exuberant to get this email, thanking God for making my heart glad and for my glory to rejoice in hope. I immediately filled out the form and forwarded it to them. Psalm 16:8-9 "I have set the Lord always before me; because He is at my right hand, I shall not be moved. Therefore, my heart is glad, and my glory rejoices; my flesh also will rest in hope." Remaining hopeful in God, I expected the check to arrive soon.

I kept my Lord first in my life and diligently decided to observe the Daniel fast, which drew me closer to God. I was walking through a phase of trials and tribulations and was under a severe attack from Satan. It was spiritual warfare. All my plans to glorify God were either getting blocked, delayed, or destroyed. I had my website in America, but I had to close it as I was moving back to India.

I had lost all my subscribers and my connections, and it was in my heart to build a new website again. I Google searched for companies that would do it for me and suddenly got a call from Tiara Digital. The gentleman on call was very polite and asked me if he could come over to discuss my project with me. When he arrived, he saw all my write-ups, fliers, and pictures and heard my songs. He was very enthusiastic to work for me. I asked him about his price, but he suggested that he would be able to give me the right quotation after thoroughly studying the entire project. Then, after having a long conversation over a cup of coffee, he suggested that he would need all of my CDs, write-ups, and photos to start my work. I handed him all of it, and he left. Time passed by, and he never got back to me, devouring all my precious stuff. Then, I assigned another company where Mr. Gawde signed an agreement with me to finish my work in eight weeks. He worked for a few weeks to get his first installment of Rs 5000 and then played a dirty game by giving false promises and false pretexts about being ill and deaths in his family. The other Studio that I hired worked for a long time but closed its business due to Covid and disappeared into thin air after receiving Rs 10000 from me.

I was done - and saddened. But in my spirit, I knew God would not put me to shame, and in His perfect time, He would get me a capable Christian believer to make my website. Romans 8:28, "For we know that all things work together for your good to those who love God, for those who are called according to His purpose." I kept pondering and looking for ways to do things on my own by searching prestigious companies, but I chose none to make my website. I tried to search by choosing another option and typing, "Freelance Graphic Designer companies in the suburbs." A huge list appeared. I browsed through it for a long time when suddenly, the spirit nudged me to call a particular number that was not of any prestigious company. The guy immediately picked up the phone and spoke with me in Hindi. He sounded very excited and enthusiastic, convincing me by blowing his own trumpet that he was well-versed in graphics and websites. As we communicated further, I asked him if he knew about Lord Jesus. He then shouted out and said in Hindi, "Yes! I am a born-again Christian, and I have just been baptized. I am a Maharashtrian, and I have accepted the Lord Jesus Christ." I asked him where he was located and found out he was just a stone's throw away from my home. He was also happy to know that and insisted that I pay a visit to his office today. The beauty of God's glory was that same day I visited his office, the day on which he had finally decided to close his office. But it was God's good will that instead of him closing his office, God sent me to inaugurate his office. I then prayed over his office and anointed it with the precious blood of Jesus, asking for promotion, prosperity, and blessing to come upon him. Then I asked him about his business name, and I was surprised to know that my name, "Kad," was already written on his office nameplate. God was on His right hand to promote him from the slums to have an office in Bandra West and to send me over there to mentor him, knowing that he had studied in a Marathi school and had no knowledge of English. It was a big struggle for me to teach him from scratch, to spell each word for him to write in English, to make him correct repeated mistakes, to teach him how to pronounce every word, and to explain its meaning in Hindi. But I never gave up, knowing that God had put me on this assignment to support and establish him. Then, I took the entire liability to set up his business and to make him settle in life. His business then prospered when He displayed my website, to all. One day, he said, "Ma'am, I was craving to do God's work, and I am blessed God gave me this opportunity to work on your website."

I kept mentoring him by teaching him how to read the Bible in English, translating its meaning into Hindi, and sharing Bible testimonies so that he may learn to lean on God and get closer to Him.

Satan then attacked us, and all of a sudden, my laptop stopped working, and his office computer was shut down. After waiting for a couple of days, we decided to visit the Maple Store to get everything fixed. As we entered the store, the supervisor greeted us and asked us about the purpose of our visit. I said, "I am here to get my laptop fixed." He pointed toward the staircase and said, "The department is down in the basement; you can go there." We went down, and the guy concerned there said, "The guy who works on the laptops is off duty today. If you wish, you can leave your number so that we can inform you about the day he will be back." I thanked him and left, and as I was climbing up the tiny spiral marble staircase, I told my assistant, "This is such a dangerous staircase that anybody can fall and fracture all their bones." A couple of days later, I got a call from the Maple Store asking me to visit them. I left immediately on my own to meet the concerned guy at the store. He checked the laptop and said, "You have a problem with your server." I told him, "You are right - it is not a server that I bought from India, but from America." He then suggested changing the server. I thanked him and left. As I was climbing up the spiral marble staircase, I fell unaware making a huge sound of "THUD," which made me fall on my left elbow. My chest was on one marble slab, my abdomen on another slab, my knees on another, and the last slab was above my feet. I was on the edge of a turning slippery corner and could have slipped down and fractured all my bones, but the angels of the Lord God picked me up in their arms. I could not even decipher how on earth I fell in the first place and how I was saved. The guys on the ground floor came rushing to pick me up. They pulled a chair to make me rest, brought water to drink, and suggested taking me to the hospital. I refused, knowing that God was in full control. I waited for a while, thanked them, and left for my home, refusing their proposal to drive me back home. When I reached home, I checked my whole body, but there was no scar, no bruise, no bleeding, and not even the slightest pain in my body. My laptop was intact and not broken, nor were there any scratches on my phone. The Bible verse says, "For He shall give His angels charge over you, to keep you in all your ways. In their hands, they shall bear you up so that you will not dash your foot against a stone." Psalm 91:11-12.

God's mercies are new each day, and that was the day he saved me.

When I shared this testimony with my assistant, he said, "Ma'am, you only prophesied about the fall, and you, yourself, fell down. Whatever you say always turns out to be true." Then we both had a hearty laugh, and I told him, "I said anybody can fall, not me." We both giggled a lot, simultaneously thanking God for His goodness.

My life's journey has been about my personal relationship with God; if He had not been in the midst of my heart and mind, my life would have been void. His purpose for my life kept transforming me into the person He wanted me to be. Simultaneously, I aligned myself with Him to have a mind of Christ (an ability to make decisions) as He would for me. It was the most exciting spiritual experience for me to wait, watch, and see how His Revelations get transformed into Reality. The apartment that I had in Mumbai was beautiful, but the problem was that I could not have Praise and Worship Home Groups and prayer meetings over there. But I waited in peace, thinking and thanking that God Jesus, who knows all about my thoughts, will one day guide me to own a permanent prayer home. As the Bible verse promises, "And the peace of God, which surpasses all understanding, will guide your hearts and minds through Lord Jesus." Philippians 4:7. Then by faith and being in peace, I claimed my thoughts to come alive, trusting that my "Thoughts are Things." It was after months that I got the answer. I had a dream. I saw myself sleeping in bed, and all of a sudden, I observed myself walking out of my bedroom – and was shocked to see that the main entrance door of my apartment was partially opened with a dual golden chain going outside my door, blocking it from being closed from inside. Then I looked above and found out that the socket of the latch above that locks the door had been removed, except the below partition portion of the latch being intact. I screamed aloud, and I woke up with a jerk and found out that I was still safe in my bed. Then, I was unable to sleep, so I tossed and turned in my bed, feeling restless. I kept on rewinding the whole episode in my mind, repeatedly seeking answers about its clue. Finally, I got the answer that it was the Lord's signal to open my house door for me - to let me move on - out of this apartment.

The Story Begins with an Amazing Testimony.

I had a beautiful bungalow in America with a huge backyard where I could walk and talk with neighbors and relax during the evening hours. I left that behind, making it history. But to think about a bungalow in Mumbai was a fantasy. Although I had a beautiful apartment in Mumbai, I was still deprived of the freedom to walk, chat, and fellowship with neighbors that I had in America, where no houses had boundaries. While here in Mumbai, all are locked in their own apartments, and I felt like a caged bird whose feathers had been ripped off and who could fly no more. But Lord knew more than I can imagine of all that was going on within me, and on one fine morning, I received a call from a lady called Neelam, and she said, "Ma'am, our new building is under construction in Goregaon, and I believe you were looking for a property to buy. I called you to pay a visit there." Then I told her, "How did you get my number? Who said I was looking for property in Goregaon? It is so far; why would I want to buy a property there." But she kept on insisting, explaining that it's not far from the suburbs, the new road is under construction, and it is close to both International and Domestic airports. We have 34 amenities in our building, like a swimming pool, terrace garden restaurants, cafeteria, party halls, all sorts of indoor as well as outdoor games, kids garden, seniors walk pathway, library, Indoor theatre to watch movies, complimentary clubhouse membership, and a recording studio. When she said recording studio, the bell rang! Then she said, "Ma'am, please visit us and have a look today. I will arrange for a cab to pick you up and drop you off." I told her, "It's very short notice," but she said, "Ma'am, please come, don't miss this opportunity. Please come at 1 p.m. and say yes, then I will book the cab and inform you.'

Then I forwarded her my residential address on WhatsApp, confirming that it was yes, and started sorting things to get ready. By 1 p.m. sharp, the cab arrived below my residence. Then we drove off, and when I reached there, I saw the huge, classy hall and lots of people seated at round tables negotiating with the other lady representatives. Then a lady walked up to me and asked, "Ma'am, what are you looking for?" and I told her, "I am looking for a restroom to wash my hands." She then walked me through it, and as I was washing my hands, she asked me if I was a film artist. I then replied, "I am an International Gospel Singer."

As we returned back to the hall, she mentioned her uncle's name, and I asked her if she knew Pradeep Pundit. She said, "Oh my God, his daughter is married to my brother; you are like a family to me now." She then got a call from Neelam, and while speaking to her, she said, "Yes, Kadambari has arrived, and she is here with me. I will do the needful." Then she ordered coffee and showed me a big booklet of amenities and the price quotations of different-sized apartments. I then told her, "The price is too high, I don't have a budget for that, and I will not be able to buy this property." Then she took me to her private cabin where the office boy brought her a hot lunch tiffin. She insisted that I have that meal with her, but I refused her a couple of times. Then she said, "I will also not have lunch if you don't have it with me. If you have lunch with me, then I will give you a good discount, stating that you are my family member." We both chatted and then had lunch together. Then she took me to the main manager's cabin and introduced me as her relative to him. Then we sat down and negotiated for a long time. The manager then promised that he would give me the privilege of getting the best parking facility at the podium nearest to my entry gate. I looked at all the documents and then swiped my card and paid them the booking amount of Rs 100000. Then, I signed the contract document and received a scanned copy of my payments from them. The cab was waiting for me, and then I drove back home. When I reached home, I reminisced about the whole episode being in a trance and fell at the Lord's feet, crying and thanking Him for His amazing gift that He gave me by turning that bad event outcome of America back into a good outcome by placing me in a palatial apartment to enjoy all sorts of 34 amenities that anyone could ever imagine. How awesome is He?

CHAPTER 23

FOURTEEN PRECIOUS YEARS STOLEN

My marriage was a bad event that stole fourteen precious years of my life that can never be retrieved. For our life is a one-time, earthly gift from God, to live life to the brim, to cherish, to enjoy, to spend quality time with family, to thank the Lord for all His goodness, and for the opportunity He gave us, to admire His magnanimous creation, power, glory, and splendor.

I was blessed to enjoy maximum quality time with my Lord, who brought in abundant testimonies to glorify His name. But, on the other hand, my married life had no quality time testimonies, except the crucifixion testimony of Jesus on the Cross. Just as Jesus Christ paid the price for our sins, similarly, I also paid the price for my husband's sin, being a sacrificial lamb to be tortured. The Bible verse says, "Husbands love your wives, and do not be harsh with them." Colossians 3:19.

We live in a fallen, sinful world where husbands fail to recognize the value of their wives, and as a result, their wicked, sinful nature brings dishonor and disrespect to the Mighty Lord.

The Lord then commanded me and said, "Leave for Mumbai immediately," and brought me out from the clutches of the sinful marital bond, exactly as He brought the Israelites out from the bondage of the wicked Egyptians. He knew that the in-between marriage period of my survival with the Egyptian of my life was none other than a real waste of time, energy, and a useless effort to change my husband's mind and heart. A worthless season for me to sow on a dirty, miry, dry soil to reap nothing but a foolish struggle to face the storms to reap the thorns. The Bible verse says, "When you spread out your hands, I will hide My eyes from you; even thou you make many prayers, I will not hear. Your hands are full of blood." Isaiah 1:15.

The Lord's covenant vows demand man to be faithful to his wife, but sinners' hands are full of blood. Their punishment is that God detests them and refuses to hear their prayers. He knows most men are not faithful to their wives and fail to pay their vows. The marriage vows made on the altar implicate the covenant vow that the Lord had made with humanity. "I am with you even unto the end of the world." Marriage is a one-time, special, sacred event in a man's life to be remembered forever. Marriage is a dream of each person, an inborn inner desire, and a search to find someone who meets your heart's expectations to live happily ever after. It's also a leap of faith into a new journey of excitement, fun, joy, and love. A marriage that obtains favor from God can be successful when two imperfect partners follow God's Covenant vows and refuse to give up on each other, leaving aside all their choices and preferences.

Marriage is also a jackpot, for one in a million, when out of nowhere, love gives a fairy tale excitement by being cuddled in the arms of the right buddy, that gives you warmth, security, and assurance that you are someone, precious, special, and loved. The positive vibes of assurance then fills the heart with gratitude to thank God for His goodness in bringing the right man/wife into your life.

A happy marriage is part of everyone's wish. I also expected to have a happy marriage that would stand on pillars of a strong bond, cemented with a covenant-abiding commitment that pleases God. The Bible verse says, "He who finds a wife finds a good thing and obtains favor from the Lord." Proverbs 18:22. A wife is a gift of God to a man, and the quality that man brings into the marriage is a gift to God.

Marriage is a lifelong journey of learning to love like Christ. A journey that thrives on love, respect, communication, trust, and patience. Love is the basic tool in marriage. It recognizes no barriers. It can jump hurdles, it can walk through the fire, it can jump fences, and it can cross borders to win the heart of the beloved one. Loving someone deeply gives you satisfaction and joy, and being loved by someone gives you the assurance that you are the "only one my life, my wife."

God does not require marriage to be a one-night stand, a temporary ritual, but He wants the marriage relationship to evolve and go fonder, exactly as His unconditional, agape love forever. The best tool for that is to use God's love language in marriage to earn trust, favor, and respect from each other. The Bible verse says, "When thou shall vow a vow unto the Lord thy God, thou shall not slack to pay it; for the Lord thy God will surely require it of thee, and it would be sin in thee." Deuteronomy 23:21.

Gradually, marriage stands the test of time to prove its worth when both partners stay closer in happy times and unhappy times, in joy and in pain, in prosperity and in poverty, in seasons or without reasons.

Unfortunately, my husband never stood with me during any season or without any reason. All I can say is that he is answerable to the Lord. The Bible verse says, "God does not hear sinners; but if anyone is a worshipper of God and does His will, He hears him." John 9:31. Thus trusting the Lord's promise that he would hear my prayer. I paid my husband's vows by continuously praying for him.

CHAPTER 24

PRAYER PETITION FOR MY HUSBAND

"Hear my prayer, O LORD, and let my cry come to You. Do not hide Your face from me in the day of trouble; incline Your ear to me; In the day that I call, answer me speedily."

– Psalm 102:1-2

I loved my husband and trusted him to be my best friend, my best soul mate, and to be a man of God. It was our God-designed marriage… a covenant made before God to bring us together both spiritually and physically-where infidelity and divorce had no space to survive in our holy bond.

The Bible verse says, "If your right eye causes you to sin, pluck it out and cast it from you; for it is more profitable for you that one of your members perish, than for your whole body to be cast into hell." Matthew 5:29

My husband was a strong believer in the Lord and was well-versed in all the Biblical stories and scriptures that he read. He was a dedicated man after God and loved serving God by preaching the Word of God to a group of his co-workers in his head office and to the prayer group in our local church in Wisconsin, where we regularly attended the Sunday Church Service.

Having been married to a man of God, I always felt safe living happily ever after with him till death set us apart. But I was wrong and naive, not knowing that my own husband, my faithful companion, would turn out to be the 'Judas' of my life, to betray me, similarly to the Judas of the Bible, who betrayed Jesus.

It was Sunday morning, the day of my betrayal, when I had left my home in a jiffy, and when I reached the church, I went to the restroom to comb my hair while my husband waited in the prayer room. After a few minutes, I left and walked back up to the prayer room, and found my husband slyly texting his friend on his cell without even noticing my presence. But, as soon as he heard the sound of my high heels, his face immediately changed color. He got confused and confounded and quickly hid his phone behind his back. I asked him, "What is the matter? Why are you trying to hide your cell from me? Show me your cell." Then, immediately, he got up from his chair and swiftly left for the restroom, saying, "Nothing." The church service had already started, and later, he entered and said, "You can check my phone." I replied to him and said, "I am not interested in checking your phone, nor am I interested in knowing about your sly activities. It's between you and the Lord to judge. I am out."

All through the church service, I was disturbed and perplexed by the unexpected situation, which created emotions of pain, unrest, and hurt within me. I was unable to pay attention, to focus on the pastor's message, being mentally perplexed to weather this sudden, turbulent thunderstorm in my life.

Moreover, I was extremely saddened that instead of praying to the Lord in the church prayer room, David focused on his heart's call to appease himself. Church is a sacred place where we go each Sunday to revere and thank God and to render praises for all the good things that God has blessed us with. Our allegiance is towards God, but by his sly act, he not only disgraced me as his wife but also brought dishonor to our God by cheating on me right in front of the Lord's eyes, who ponders all the paths of a man.

The Bible verse says, "Vows made to You are binding upon me, O God; I will render praises to You." Psalm 56:12-13

Sin may look very enticing, appeasing, and exciting to a man initially, but the Bible verse says, "For the ways of the man are before the eyes of the Lord, and He ponders all his paths. His own iniquities entrap the wicked man, and he is caught in the cords of his own sin. He shall die for lack of instruction of his folly, and he shall go astray." Proverbs 5:21-23

I respected my husband, holding him in high esteem to be worthy of status and to be called a faithful man of God. But to accept and acknowledge his immoral conduct to be anything less than a sin would have been my disobedience towards God and a disgrace to my own self. By that time, I was also fully aware that he had been a victim of a severe addiction.

For months, I had been repulsed, watching him being engrossed till late at night on his laptop watching disgusting stuff. I spent sleepless nights of solidarity on my bed, turning and tossing in despair as to how David, a man of God, could have gotten trapped in Satan's lust, knowing that by doing so, he would create enmity with God.

"Adulterers and adulteress! Do you not know that friendship with the world is enmity with God? Whosoever wants to be a friend of the world makes himself an enemy of God." James 4:4

Then, I expressed my emotions of sorrow to the Lord and petitioned Him to empower me with wisdom to save my husband from his addiction. But the Spirit nudged me, "You will have to deal with two Egyptians of your life. The first Egyptian is your husband, and the second Egyptian is Satan, the one who rules over your husband's mind by trapping him in his own clutches."

The Bible verse says, "Confess your trespasses to one another, and pray for one another, that you may be healed. The effective, fervent prayer of a righteous man avails much." James 5:16

I knew that my husband would neither confess nor partner with me in prayers. Then, I humbled myself, crying to the Lord through fervent prayers and petitions to save him. The Holy Spirit then led me to follow the Bible's instructions to save my husband. So, being strong, through God's power, I confronted him, saying, "Nothing is hidden from me, and I am fully aware of your addiction. I know what all you have been watching till late hours at night on your laptop." Then, according to the second Bible instruction, the next morning, I went ahead to meet the elder of our church to report to him that my marriage was at stake due to my husband's affair and addiction. I also told him he is a man of God, but somehow Satan has intervened to break our marriage so that my gospel ministry may suffer. "Please kindly help me," I pleaded. Then the elder said, "I will ask your husband to meet me tomorrow to discuss further with him." I then thanked him and left the church.

The elder then called David over to his church and made arrangements for our counseling session with a counselor who was close to our street. Then, the next early morning, we both reached the counselor's office. My husband was called in first while I waited for him in the reception room. Then, I was called in, and the counselor asked me a couple of questions regarding my husband. I told him the truth, stating, "My husband has been having an affair with someone and has been cheating on me for a long time." Then, immediately, my husband shouted out and said, "I am not having any affair with anyone," and bluntly told the counselor, "The truth is, I have no emotion in this marriage. I was not in love with my wife when I married her. Then how can I love her now after marriage?"

My whole world turned upside-down as I heard him speak those disgraceful words to demean me. I immediately got up, left the room, and wept bitterly in the restroom.

The Bible verse says, "If an enemy were insulting me, I could endure it; if a foe was rising against me, I could hide. But it is you, a man like myself, my companion, my close friend, with whom I have enjoyed "Sweet Fellowship" at the house of God as we walked among the worshippers." Psalm 55:12-14

I knew David detested me because I had failed to be a good wife who should have participated and covered his sins. But instead of doing so, when he got to know that I had approached the church elder, he was extremely bugged with me and shouted out, "You have opened a can of worms for me." I then said, "At least now, the filthy worms will be out of your life." I did my uttermost to save my husband for his own good, but he hated me, assuming that I was defaming him. I knew the truth that it was the Devil who had been trying hard to steal our marriage. He did all that to stop my gospel ministry, by getting me engrossed in shame and grief, by destroying our marital life by entrapping my husband, to cause him to sin. I then started searching for Bible scriptures to save my husband from the wages of sin.

Then, when I read about all the wages of sin of God, it gripped me in fear. The tears kept streaming down from my eyes as I kept writing the following scripture verses in my book about the loss and final destiny of a sinner.

HIS PRAYER IS AN ABOMINATION TO GOD

"One who turns away his ear from hearing the law, even his Prayer, is an abomination."

– Proverbs 28:9

HE IS SEPARATED FROM GOD

But your iniquities have made a separation between you and your God, and your sins have hidden His face from you so that he does not hear."

– Isaiah 59:2

HIS SOUL IS DESTROYED

"Whoever commits adultery with a woman lacks understanding; he who does so destroys his soul."

– Proverbs 6:32

HE WILL NOT PROSPER

"He who covers his sins will not prosper, but whosoever confesses and forsakes them will have mercy."

– Proverbs 28:13

HE LOSES ETERNAL LIFE IN CHRIST

"For the wages of sin is death, but the free gift of God is eternal life in Christ Jesus our Lord."

– Romans 6:23

HE WILL BE GUILTY & HIS PRAYER SIN

"When he is judged, let him be found guilty, and let his prayer become sin."

– Psalm 109:7

The power of God's love is the center of relationships and marriage. When husband and wife come together in holy matrimony, they commit to God's plan for their life. They know that Christ paid the price with His precious blood to redeem us from sin to receive the free gift of eternal life. But my husband nullified God's plan for our married life and preferred to opt for his earthly plan to appease his flesh.

Then, according to God's command, I finally left for India, never to return back to him. I destroyed the return ticket and threw it into the dustbin, suggesting him to proceed ahead with divorce that you really deserve from my end. And he finally succeeded in breaking his own home. The Bible verse says, "But everyone who hears these words of mine and does not put them into practice is like a 'foolish man' who built his house on sand. The rain came down, the streams rose, and the wind blew and beat against that house, and it fell with a great crash." Matthew 7:26

CHAPTER 25

SATAN SUCCEEDED TO DESTROY MY MARRIAGE

BY ENTRAPPING MY HUSBAND

Satan has been the enemy of God and marriage since the beginning. He hates marriage because marriage is a portrayal of the gospel. Satan opposes the gospel by seeking to keep man away from salvation in Jesus Christ. The Bible verse says, "Now the parable is this: The seed is the Word of God. Those by the wayside are the ones who hear then the devil comes and takes away the word out of their hearts, lest they should believe and be saved." Luke 8:11-12. Satan never wanted us to be saved and have eternal life in Jesus Christ because Satan has been an untiring, unceasing adversary of God and His people. His plan of rebellion in action has been endless, to turn the order and authority upside down to subvert God's plan in marriage. Thus, he manipulated Adam through Eve to eat the forbidden fruit from the Tree of Life and succeeded in bringing their fall, which destroyed their relationship with God.

Jesus says in Matthew 12:25-26 "Every kingdom divided against itself is brought to desolation, and every city and house divided against itself will not stand." If Satan casts out Satan, he is divided against himself. How, then, will his kingdom stand?

Then, to make his kingdom stand, he schemed to make families frail so that they would not become fruitful. His cunning strategy to attack marriage was a way of family destruction to bring desolation by diverting the mind of the man, to get him entrapped and tempted to appease his own flesh so that his soul may be destroyed.

His purpose was and is to turn the order and authority of God upside down by taking authority over man's mind to destroy his soul and to darken his understanding that he may fail to relish and register his wife's sincere love of true sacrifice and service, so that he may be alienated from the life of God's purpose for his happy married life.

> *The Bible verses say, "Whosoever commits adultery with a woman lacks understanding; he who does so destroys his soul."*
>
> **– Proverbs 6:32**

SATAN DEPRIVES MAN OF INHERITING THE KINGDOM OF GOD.

Satan's plan to make man sin is like an undercurrent in the ocean; if you are lured in its lust, you will be empowered and carried away to destruction by disinheriting the Kingdom of God.

The Bible verse says, "For this you know, that no fornicator, unclean person, nor the covetous man, who is idolater has any inheritance in the kingdom of Christ and God."

– Ephesians 5:5

SATAN DEPRIVES MAN TO SERVE GOD

He makes man unholy by involving him in sexual lust by demeaning him to be unacceptable in the sight of God.

The Bible verse says, "I BESEECH you therefore, brethren, by the mercies of God, that you present your bodies a living sacrifice, holy acceptable to God, which is your reasonable service."

– Romans 12:1

SATAN MAKES MAN AN ENEMY OF THE CROSS

A man whose allegiance is towards his own flesh to satisfy him, with the lust of the world, makes himself the enemy of the Cross.

The Bible verse says, "For many walk, of whom I have told you often, and now tell you even weeping, that they are enemies of the Cross."

– Philippians 3:18

SATAN DESTROYS MAN'S GLORY INTO SHAME

Satan destroys the life of man by luring him into the path of darkness and setting his mind on earthly things to put him to shame.

The Bible verse says, "Whose end is destruction, whose god is their belly, and whose glory is in their shame… who set their mind on earthly things."

– Philippians 3:19

SATAN CORRUPTS MAN TO SIN IN SECRECY

Secrecy is another tactic of Satan to corrupt man's thought process by involving him in sexual sins, which convinces him to be a much-wanted sweet chocolate cake with girls hovering over him. That broadens his shoulders and makes him seem like a superhero. But in reality, Satan makes him a weaker, worthless vessel in the site of the Lord to be doomed to death.

The Bible verses say, "If a man commits adultery with another man's wife… with the wife of his neighbor… both adulterer and adulteress must be put to death."

– Leviticus 20:20

"Do not lust after her beauty in your heart, nor let her allure you with her eyelids. For the means of the harlot, a man is reduced to the crust of bread, and an adulteress will prey upon his precious life. Can a man take fire to his bosom and his clothes not be burned? Can one walk on hot coals and his feet not be seared?"

– Proverbs 6:25-28

"Remove your way far from her and do not go near the door of her house, lest you give your honor to others, and your years to the cruel one, lest aliens be filled with your wealth, and your labors go to the house of a foreigner; and you mourn at last when your flesh and body are consumed.

– Proverbs 5:8-14

"Now, therefore, listen to me, my children; pay attention to the words of my mouth: Do not let your heart turn aside to her ways; do not stray into her paths. For she had cast down many wounded, and all who were slain by her were strong men. Her house is a way to hell, descending down to the chambers of death."

– Proverbs 7:24-27

CHAPTER 26

GOD'S PURPOSE FOR MARRIAGE

Marriage should be honored by all, and the marriage bed kept pure.

– Hebrews 13:4

SENSIBLE HUSBAND ENJOYS THE GIFT OF GOD

HE CELEBRATES EACH DAY WITH HIS WIFE.

A sensible married husband knows each day is a gift of God to celebrate, to love life, and to enjoy the good things of life.

HE OBTAINS FAVOR FROM GOD.

The Bible verse says, "He who finds a wife finds a good thing and obtains favor from the Lord."

– Proverbs 18:22

HIS PLEASANT WORDS ARE LIKE A HONEYCOMB TO HIS WIFE.

"A man has joy by the answer of his mouth and a word spoken in due season."

– Proverbs 15:23

The Bible verse says, "Pleasant words are like a honeycomb, sweetness to the soul and health to the bones."

– Proverbs 16:24

HE MAKES EACH DAY JOYFUL FOR HIS WIFE.

A sensible husband makes it a point that his speech should always be seasoned with salt and that his wife's day should be joyful and pleasant.

"Let your speech always be with grace, seasoned with salt, that you may know how you ought to answer each other."

– Colossians 4:6

HIS WORDS OF LOVE ARE LIKE PRECIOUS JEWELS TO HIS WIFE.

"There is gold and a multitude of rubies, but the lips of knowledge are a precious jewel."

– Proverbs 20:15

HIS FOUNTAIN IS BLESSED TO REJOICE WITH HIS WIFE.

"Let your fountain be blessed, and rejoice with the wife of your youth."

– Proverbs 5:18

HIS RIGHT ANSWER IS LIKE A KISS TO HIS WIFE.

"He who gives a right answer kisses the lips."

– Proverbs 24:26

HIS PRAYER IS TO SING PRAISES TO GOD

"May my tongue sing of your word, for all your commands are righteous."

– Psalm 119:172

CHAPTER 27

FOOLISH HUSBAND DESTROYS HIS MARRIAGE

"The Lips of the Fools Bring Strife, And their Mouths Invite Beatings"

– Proverbs 18:6

"To you, O men, I call, and my voice is to the sons of men. The fear of the Lord is to hate evil; pride and arrogance and the evil way the perverse mouth I hate."

– Proverbs 8:4,13

HE PURSES HIS LIPS TO BRING EVIL.

"He winks his eyes to devise perverse things and purses his lips to bring evil."

– Proverbs 16:30

HE DOES NOT UNDERSTAND THE WILL OF GOD.

"Therefore, do not be unwise, but understand what the will of the Lord is."

– Ephesians 5:17

HIS EVIL IS ON HIS LIPS LIKE A BURNING FIRE.

"An ungodly man digs up evil, and it is on his lips like a burning fire."

– Proverbs 16:27

HE SOWS DISCORD, AND SUDDENLY, HE SHALL BE BROKEN WITHOUT REMEDY.

"Perversity is in his heart, he devises evil continuously, and he sows discord. Therefore, calamity shall come suddenly; suddenly, he shall be broken without remedy."

– Proverbs 6:14-15

HE PRACTICES DECEIT, AND POISON IS UNDER HIS LIPS.

"Their throat is an open tomb; with their tongues, they have practiced deceit; The poison of asps is under their lips."

– Romans 3:13

"God will judge the adulterer and all sexually immoral."

– Hebrews 13:4

LOVE LETTERS

The Initial Charm of My Godly, Sensible Husband A Collection of Letters

Hi Babe,

I am missing you every day. The house is always so empty and quiet. I watch TV and play the games but that grows old. I am now starting to work in the basement so that will be something different to do. I love you, my lovely wife and I think about you, believing that you being there away from home is God's will and for His purposes. I am still very excited about your trip starting in June knowing you will be a huge blessing to all those people in Australia, and especially in Fiji. Bye for now. Know I love you and miss you. Being home alone every night makes me miss you and your love for me. I love you babe very much. Hmm. Hmm

Yours,

David

Hi My Sweetie

How do I love you-----------Tremendously.

When do I love you----------Always.

Together let's raise our glasses and toast this wonderful union that God has given us. You are my wife, lover and friend. Be comforted by knowing that I am being a good boy here waiting patiently for you. I am growing closer to the Lord and laying hold of Him praying for your safety, anointing and power to minister to the people, wisdom, strength, peace and every good. Come home soon. I love you and miss you a lot.

Forever Yours,

David

Greetings to my precious wife Kads,

HAPPY BIRTHDAY SWEETIE!!!!!

By the time you are reading this, your birthday has already come, and we have clinked our glasses together on the phone in recognition and celebration of the event. It is too bad we are not able to celebrate in person, but we know that our separation is for the Lord's work. That fact does not make the long days without you go any better, however.

It has been a long cold and difficult winter to cope with alone. When you are here, I have my true best friend and companion and the days are much better when I can come home to your smiling face. I hope that you will be planning to come home by the end of April as we have been talking about. I will be truly disappointed if you are delayed past that unless you have concerts scheduled that would delay it a little longer.

Once again Happy Birthday to you. I miss you so very much and I love you and appreciate you as my wife, friend, and lover.

With all of my love and care.

Love you, Love you, Love you,

David

To my lovely wife Kads,

HAPPY VALENTINE'S DAY SWEETIE!

One touch,

One kiss,

One moment with you…

And I fall in love all over again.

Each day you are in my heart and mind.

I miss you so much.

I continue to grow in love and appreciation for you.

My heart is forever yours.

Your hubby,

David

I pray and thank my so-called husband, who withheld all the goodness from me. My marital rites, love, respect, integrity, companionship, peace, joy, contentment, happiness, and my alimony and pension funds. Finally, I bid him adieu. May the Lord God Almighty bless him.

The Bible verse says, "Love your enemies, do good to those who hate you, bless those who curse you, and pray for those who hurt you." Luke 6:27-28

CHAPTER 28

MY MARRIAGE RESERVOIR

Narcissist Personality Disorder

Matthew 10:36: "And a man's enemies will be those of his household."

That is so true! My ex's tongue was a volume of treasure, silver, gold, pearls, rubies, and diamonds, that he showered on me by filling in our Marriage Reservoir to satisfy his heart's yearnings.

THE TREASURES OF OUR PRECIOUS RESERVOIR

You are my wife because we stay under the same roof.

I am what I am; I cannot change myself.

Even if I give up everything, still nothing will change in our relationship.

I am happy in America, and you would be much happier in India.

You can think what you want. I don't give a damn.

HIS CRUELTY KNEW NO BOUNDS

Why are you thrusting food on my plate? I will eat what I want. (It's a gesture of love and respect according to the Indian culture to serve food with your own hands to your husband, family, or guest, for which he said I was being discourteous to him.)

After his leg surgery on both legs, he went golfing and was exhausted, having acute pain. I offered for him to sit on the couch, as he was uncomfortable sitting on a kid's stool. Then he and his relative both said I was "disrespectful" to him… All my Indian culture's courtesies were unmannerly in his sight. For this reason, he made me shed tears for years.

I have my life to live the way I want and how I want- I have decided, period.

Why should I join you for your ministry work? It's your calling, not my calling.

Why are you wasting your money on me by buying me expensive Armani suits? This is not my love language.

I don't see things the way you see them.

Why would you decorate my house? I like it just the way it is.

The curtains you stitched don't match the furniture. I don't like them. I don't see them the way you see them.

Do you want to go to Saudi Arabia, where a man chopped off his wife's head? He said that while we were watching the same cruel incident on TV.

He spoiled every trip of mine and tried his best to hurt me with his venom. When we were driving on a highway we observed a charred burned house, and he said, "Do you want to stay in that burned house that we just saw on the highway?

When he observed a graveyard on one of our trips, he said, "Do you want to go to the graveyard that we just passed?" He took every opportunity to gaslight me.

When we were watching the live tragic news on PBS, of an American plane whose door had fallen out, he said, "What if this door had fallen on your head?" I replied, "It would be your loss to pay the huge hospital bills for me."

The Bible verse says, "On the lips of him who has understanding, wisdom is found, but a rod is for the back of him who lacks sense." Proverbs 10:13.

I have no vision for the vision that you have. I am not sitting here to promote you.

It's not my job to do that.

Why would I join you for your concerts? It's your calling, not mine.

I am not interested in music.

I am not going to sit and crib if you don't return from India.

I have a new strategy to change my attitude. I will tell you when the right time arrives.

When we were out on one of our trips, we observed a huge asylum. He said, "Do you want to go to the mental asylum?" That was the time; I answered him back and said, "Yes, when you take me in there, and when the Dr. sees my classy looks and sophisticated personality, he surely will think you are a deranged man and will rather admit you in the asylum. And much more of his rubbish, and bla bla bla…

He never stood by my side to shoulder my burdens, neither encouraged me to pursue my singing talent nor supported my business proposal to start the Indian Cuisine Restaurant in America.

In fourteen years of my married life, he never accompanied me for a single concert nor desired to know how, through my songs and testimonies, I had been sowing seeds diligently to reap the fruits for God's glory. He never paid attention to what would make me feel cherished, never complimented me, never went for a walk with me, never sat to pray with me, nor took me out for a date, movie, match, or concert. He never shared his life with me in any area of his life, nor did he desire to be a part of my team. He never created a safe space for open dialogue to take place between us. His every word spoken was full of hatred, and he went out to the extent that I die. Then, one fine morning, he walked back from the office unexpectedly and started searching for something; then I asked him, "What happened?" Then he answered back and said, "When you die, I will write on your tombstone, 'What happened?'" And then he left for his office. His brutality had no bounds. He planned to snatch my joy each day, and when he read my book prior to its release, he said, "My brother will shred you into bits - you don't know how to write."The Holy Spirit then pacified my hurting soul through this verse. "A good man out of the good treasure of his heart brings forth good things, and an evil man out of the evil treasures brings forth evil things. But I say to you that for every idle word men may speak, they will give an account of it in the day of judgment. Matthew 12:35-36

The man I married I trusted was a man of God, but his traits proved that he was none other than a hardcore narcissist. Somehow, after my divorce, unexpected emails kept coming to me from the Quora Digest Magazine describing the horror stories of women who had been tortured by narcissistic husbands… stating narc's traits, that their husbands are in search of supply, they are partner hoppers, and they use the tactic of the silent treatment to avoid, disrespect, and demean their wife, and they emotionally abuse their wife by gaslighting.

The other article stated that individuals with Narcissist Personality Disorder have been found to have less volume of grey matter in the left anterior insula, a part related to empathy, emotional regulation, compassion, and cognitive functioning. They are misogynists who hold women in contempt. They loathe their wives and seek to torment and frustrate them, either by debasing them sexually or withholding sex from them. I was shocked to know that Quora Digest had finally solved my lifelong puzzle, for which I had been struggling for years, to find out why my husband hates and loathes me so… much.

"Useless wrangling of men of corrupt minds and destitute of the truth that supposes godliness is a means of gain. Even from such, withdraw yourself." 1Timothy 6:5

I had already withdrawn myself following the Lord's command and had obtained a permanent no contact passport.

When you generate issues in your life, you also invent the results you deserve to reap a punishment for yourself. Punishment then deprives you of the emotions to love and hug your own wife. The 'God-given gift to you.' The status that God grants you then is of a still mannequin statue, to be relegated in the corner of your own house, having been ripped off the title 'Husband," an empty, useless, inhumane vessel, void of emotions, "who knows not that everyone who loves is born of God, and knows God." But disgrace is the portion of the one who is unaware that God is love, and love is God. The emotion of love is a stimulus that automatically brings a beautiful response. They are feelings that allow us to enjoy the beauty of life as they come from the core of our hearts. If you ignore those feelings, they cry out and die, but if you relish them, they flourish to nourish you forever. There was too much love in my heart, being a child of God, who taught me the value of love by sacrificing His son for me. Then how could I not have obeyed the statutes of God to love my husband? Life is a one-time blessing to all. It's short, as time flies away fast, and there is no space even to waste a single moment. The unfortunate ones waste their life in search of supply, for they believe that variety is the spice of life, for their insatiable lust, which ultimately crushes them to the crust of bread. But they are the losers who deny themselves to avail the treasure of God's unfailing, unmerited love. Finally, they are answerable to three things when they stand before the judgment seat of the Lord: How much you loved God, how you lived according to God's commandments to fulfill His purpose, and how much you served God enduring afflictions.

For me, enduring trials and winning through wounds surely was a painful process. But for those in faith who know how to wait on the Lord, pain surely proves to be a source of joy. Just like the scars that pained my heart, later proved to me to be worthy jewels that taught me a lifetime's lessons, to know my worth, my strength, and power, to invent happiness within me.

"My brethren, count it all joy when you fall into various trials, knowing that the testing of your faith produces patience." James 1:2-4

Then I started my count to joy, deleted all the trial treasures, and threw them into the dustbin that my ex had accused and said, "That you are the one who misconstrued all that I had said to you. You are my wife, and even in the wildest dreams, I cannot even think to hurt you." Then I picked up the sacred marriage reservoir, in which he had spit venom, and flushed it down the toilet.

Having pitied him, I felt sorry for his condition, that having all of God's blessings of security, peace, happiness, love, and a joyful relationship with God, he lost everything. His gift from God, his wife, his funds, and his privilege to serve God. But I do pray that the Lord God Almighty would forgive him, bring him to repentance, and save his precious soul.

Forgiveness was my last gift to him, and moving on forward was my best gift to me.

Every person brings happiness in life. Some by entry and some by exit.

My ex's exit from my life opened a new path for me to be in the presence of God, where there was fullness of joy and pleasures in store forevermore. The Spirit within me then spoke and said, "Jesus tasted vinegar for you, that you should taste wine now, and said, "It is finished," that you should say now, "It has started."

"You make known to me the path of life; in your presence, there is fullness of joy; at your right hand are pleasures forevermore. Psalm 16:11

The transition of my new path was in God's promise that He had spoken to me years back prior to my divorce. "Blessings, I will bless you. Your cup shall run over. Now, when you go to Mumbai, go and serve the needy and the poor, and then I will give you the desires of your heart."

"Every good gift and every perfect gift is from above, coming down from the Father of the heavenly lights, who does not change like shifting shadows." James 1:6

So true! God is the same today, tomorrow, and forevermore. He never changes. Surely, His perfect gift came from above, from the Father of the heavenly lights, which was unbelievable.

"But as it is written: Eye has not seen, nor ear heard, nor have entered into the heart on man the things which God has prepared for those who love Him." Corinthians 2:9

The petals of God's promise unfurled the truth. His perfect gift came from above from the Father of heavenly lights - a breathtaking apartment having an array of 34 luxurious amenities, was ready for me to take possession. The Shepherd of my soul then walked me in. Overwhelmed by the magnitude of His love, and admiring the pious palatial apartment the tears started dripping down my eyes. I fell at His feet, kissing, worshipping, and thanking Him for this unbelievable gift, Then He lifted my chin, and His eyes met mine in a moment of spiritual intimacy, and He vanished, leaving behind His love forever.

Love became my legacy.

I launched Love-4ALL Ministry, and dedicated myself to serving, and to add value to the NGO's Ashram's 140 vulnerable souls from the streets, sick, poor, and orphaned to fulfill the Lord's commandment, for He said, "Go and serve the needy and the poor."

My ministry and dream revelation became a reality, displaying the liabilities and the facilities that the Lord had left behind for me, to enjoy in my apartment.

Soon my apartment became a humility hub, hosting prayer meetings where transformation and testimonies unfolded. Where I danced and sang aloud His praises with the worshippers to enjoy and soak in the secrets of His spiritual realm.

The indoor realm of my building was equally worth a soak that I could have ever imagined. It was self-sufficient, having all the facilities at hand. It had restaurants, a coffee shop, a terrace garden for parties, a theatre to watch movies, a library to study, a garden to chat, a gym to exercise, a recording studio and all sorts of indoor and outdoor games, a swimming pool, a walking track, Club House, etc. to enjoy all. Every area was always packed with people, with loud noises coming from the games room, the sound of music, laughter, shouts of kids, the hustle and bustle of guests, and their entry and their exit until the late hours of the night.

But the inner atmosphere in my apartment was calm and blissful, and it emanated vibes in my soul that were serene, sacred, and peaceful. The morning view from my balcony looked gorgeous as the golden orb sun rays peeped out from behind the sky's blue curtain. The chirping of the birds, the sound of the cuckoo, and the soft silky swaying of the breeze kept caressing me silently that made me say Ahah Ahah, as I sipped my morning hot cup of coffee. My heart melted, basking in joy and gratitude, reminiscing His purpose to make me enjoy posh life, surrounded by luxurious amenities to live a life of abundance.

"So is the word that goes out of my mouth; it will not return to me empty but will accomplish what I desire and achieve the purpose for which I sent you. You will go out in joy and will be led forth in peace; the mountains and the hills will burst into song before you, and the trees of the field will clap their hands."

– Isaiah 55: 11-12

"The Lord will command the blessing on you in your storehouses and in all which you set your hand, and He will bless you in the land which the Lord is giving you."

– Deuteronomy 28:8

"Arise, Shine, to the light has come, and the glory of God has risen upon thee."

– Isaiah 60:1

"The Lord your God is in the midst, a mighty one who will save; he will rejoice over you with gladness; he will quiet you with his love; he will exult over you with loud singing."

– Zephaniah 3:17

"Blessed shall you be when you come in, and blessed shall you be when you go out."

– Deuteronomy 28:6

"Then your barns will be filled to overflowing, and your vats will brim over new wine."

– Proverbs 30:10

What can I give you, Lord, in return, except to sing praises to you?

"I will praise You, Yahweh, my Elohim, with all my heart, And I will glorify Your name forevermore."

– Psalm 86:12

AMEN AMEN AMEN.

EPILOGUE

The story of my book does not end here, but as a matter of fact it starts now, as I walk gracefully into the promised glorious future to turn the tables around. I am all set and ready to write the first chapter of my new life. Having a strong conviction that my faith is stronger enough than ever to call forth my seasons to change the very course of my life. Trusting that the Lord did not make me walk through the dark tunnel without a reason. But walked me through it to see the bright light ahead, to release me to soar high into the greater heights.

His eternal word of promise that chastened me, had settled my heart in solace and serenity, to accept things that I was unable to embrace, and had given me the ability to perceive things as He would see. He bestowed the skills of knowledge, wisdom, understanding and counsel upon me to write His story in my book. His secret whispers prompted and knitted my story through dream revelations that kept me thrilled, happy, and excited to experience it's unbelievable transformation into testimonial realities. All that consumed time and years for me to complete my book. My hectic gospel tours were another reason of delay due to lack of time restraints. Simultaneously, while writing my book, Satan had been tirelessly busy to doom me. He created all sorts of obstacles to make me physically and mentally sick. He made me to walk through a very rough phase. My new Mac Pro stopped working, and also my laptop. Things became tough, and the only option I had was to write my book on my Samsung phone. The Wi-Fi interruption then kept on suddenly disrupting the signal, that vanished my written chapters. I cried and cried my heart out, to the Lord, as I had to rewrite them again. I soon suffered severe headaches and excruciating pain in my nerves, my eyes kept burning and hurting but I kept on pushing myself harder then ever, writing day in and day out. I visited three ophthalmologists, but by God's grace the reports showed positive results that my vision had improved. I then got my entire body checkups done and the report said, I had no diabetes, nor elevated blood pressure, and I was fit as a fiddle. Soon my specs glass was broken, but still I continued writing and fighting the spiritual battle, knowing fully well that it was none other, then the Satan who had been torturing me.

Finally it was on December 30th when I gained my inner confidence to challenge myself, so I humbled before the Lord. And gave myself the last ultimatum that no matter what, in Jesus name, I will finish the last chapter of my book by tomorrow morning, i.e. 31st December.

So I slept early to take a little nap on the 30th a night earlier to feel fresh. But later on that night my phone's musical message sounded, and I noticed it was 2 a.m., I then opened my bedroom window, to have my eye tonic to admire the celestial, mesmerizing beauty of the skies filled with the stars that were twinkling and shimmering like diamonds, against the darkness black of the night. Suddenly the refreshing aromatic breeze rushed in, to greet me, so that I may cherish it's rich pure dreamy bliss of wonder and mystery. I savored the beauty of that moment and was in awe of God's creation of His timeless punctuality and serenity. I was then humbled, and tears started rolling down my eyes. I knew it was now my perfect exclusive time to call upon the name of the Lord. The pious peace then dawned on me, and I saw myself being delivered into His divine destiny. I then picked up the Bible and spoke to the Lord saying, "Lord you are my God, I surrender my book to you. It's all about you and your wonders. Anoint me, bless me to finish the last chapter and reveal to me your will. I thank you, praise you, love you, and bless you." Then I closed my eyes and randomly opened the Bible to get an answer. The verse read, "Be still and know I am God; I will be exalted among the nations, I will be exalted in the earth."

Psalm 46:10.

Having this affirmation from the Lord, I was still and speechless. My joy knew no bonds. The inner calm rejuvenated my mind and soul, and my pen swiftly started writing. I simultaneously feasted my senses with the inspiring calmness of the night. The aura of tranquility, gave me mental peace and contentment, and solace and serenity gave me the opportunity to focus my mind on writing. My eyes were then very heavy and tired. I was drowsy and completely exhausted, pushing myself hard to accomplish my goal. I got then in a cheat mood, and immediately ducked myself under my soft pink blanket, to enjoy my honeydew nap for a few moments. The sleep soon caught me into her snug of mesmerizing depths that took me off to the other sphere. I found myself being escorted by the host who had thrown a lavish party to celebrate the success of his super-hit movie. The hall was lit up with lights, and with the sparkling chandeliers. The colorful blooming flowers were wrapped around all the pillars of the hall spreading the incense of its aroma. The regal touch and elegant décor created a romantic ambience. There were film producers, directors, actors, actresses, politician's, other artists, and dignitaries chatting and exchanging pleasantries. Many personalities were walking in, bringing huge bouquets of flowers, and others brought in beautifully crafted gifts.

The mesmerizing, soothing sound of melodious music was being played in the background emoting peace, joy, and love. The specialty starters were laid on the candle-lit tables and pink champagne, blue label, and wine was being served by the stewards. Soon a posh-dressed guy in a blue Armani suit walked up to me with a smiling face, who looked like a film producer. He had sported a blue sapphire diamond ring around the top of his pointy finger. He spoke to me by pointing his hand and said, "I hope you will not decline this offer." I was dazed and confounded not knowing what he meant by that, I floundered for a few moment's and replied in a jumbled mood and said, "Maybe," by shrugging back, when suddenly the musical resonance of my ticking clock awakened me. It took me quite a few moments to get back to my normal senses, as the dream had overtaken my thought's and mind. I opened my phone to continue writing and observed it was 6:00 a.m. The view outside from my window was gorgeous which took my breath away. The scenic beauty was mesmerizing, as the glittering sunrays were getting ready to paint the skies with various hues of orange, pink, yellow and gold to welcome the entry of the shimmering sun. The mango trees around my bedroom showcased its lovely red flowers and gorgeous golden ripe mangoes looked ravishing swinging to and fro by the spiralling whistling wind. The cool breeze kept lavishing its touch on my cheeks as if signaling me to connect with the Almighty. It was at that moment, I closed my eyes and worshipped the Lord, thanking, praising, and petitioning Him, to guide me through His soft whispers to make me knit the last chapter of my book. I then sat down on the chair to write. The cool blowing, breeze, brushing me, kept on inspiring me, while the sensual aroma of jasmine flower's kept on evoking my thoughts and emotions. Simultaneously the chirping of the birds, the caw caws of the crows, and the cheeps of tiny beautiful robins musical symphony created a perfect ambience. I felt my pen running fast and unstoppable, as if I was being divinely assisted to accomplish my goal and dream. I was exuberant when I finally succeeded to write the last word of my book that morning of December 31st. All that affirmed me, that God and nature were truly in tune with me, to spray the essence of God's exaltation over all the nations and on the earth. Moreover, my dream revelation coming into reality will probably be revealed in God's perfect time, when out of the blue a Godly producer will approach me to coordinate with him to make a super hit movie of my "Book's Story," to earn his merit, of being in God's Book of Fame for exalting God among all the nations, and on the earth. AMEN.

Bye for now. Hope to see you all in the cinema theatres!